RIPPLES OF LIFE

Instilling valuable life lessons

and morals in our youth

N.K. Sondhi

Rajmangal Prakashan

An Imprint of **Rajmangal Publishers**

ISBN : 978-8119251841

Published by :

Rajmangal Publishers

Rajmangal Prakashan Building,
1st Street, Ozone, Quarsi, Ramghat Road
Aligarh-202001, (UP) INDIA
Cont. No. +91- 7017993445
www.rajmangalpublishers.com
rajmangalpublishers@gmail.com
sampadak@rajmangalpublishers.in

प्रथम संस्करण : नवम्बर 2023 – पेपरबैक

प्रकाशक : राजमंगल प्रकाशन

राजमंगल प्रकाशन बिल्डिंग, 1st स्ट्रीट,

ओजोन, क्वार्सी, रामघाट रोड,

अलीगढ़, उप्र. – 202001, भारत

फ़ोन : +91 - 7017993445

First Published : Nov. 2023 - Paperback

eBook by : Rajmangal ePublishers (Digital Publishing Division)

Prelude

Life functions like an intricate echo, a cosmic reverberation where your deeds and intentions resound and return to shape your reality. Just as seeds yield their corresponding harvest, your actions sow the seeds of your destiny. The generosity you offer begets abundance, and the reflections you perceive in others, often mirror your inner essence. The symphony of life underscores the profound principle that your actions echo back faithfully, reinforcing the importance of nurturing goodwill, demonstrating respect for your elders, and radiating love towards others. These virtuous acts perpetuate a cycle of kindness, reflecting your own benevolence and missteps.

This concept unveils the Harmonies of life, encapsulating the central theme of this book. While igniting curiosity and fascination, it hints at the intricate interconnections within life and the repercussions that mould our existence. "Echoes of Existence" expands the perspective, encompassing not just individual actions but also the collective human experience, akin to sculpting the shared life experiences we encounter.

Remember, the "Life is an Echo" concept can be interpreted and expressed diversely. Depending on individual beliefs and experiences. The fundamental idea is to convey that our actions and choices carry repercussions that resonate within our lives.

The Golden Rule, often referred to as the Golden

Rule of life, encapsulates the essence of treating others with the same respect, kindness, and fairness that we desire for ourselves. This principle places a profound emphasis on empathy and consideration for the well-being of others, illuminating the interconnectedness of human experiences and relationship.

At its core, this principle encourages individuals to step into the shoes of others and contemplate how they would wish to be treated in a given situation. It serves as a moral compass, guiding ethical behavior and moral decision-making, promoting fairness, compassion, and mutual understanding. Embracing the Golden Rule acknowledges the inherent dignity of every individual, irrespective of their backgrounds, beliefs, or circumstances, fostering and environment of empathy and cooperation. Together, we strive to create a world where our treatment of others aligns with our values and desires.

Furthermore, the Golden Rule transcends cultural and religious boundaries, as variations of this principle can be found in diverse belief systems and philosophies throughout history. Its universal nature underscores its timeless wisdom and relevance in fostering harmonious relationships and social cohesion.

Fundamentally, the Golden Rule serves as a moral compass guiding us to extend kindness, respect, and fairness to others, just as we desire for ourselves. By adhering to this principle, we actively participate in the formation of a compassionate and empathetic society, wherein values of empathy and goodwill hold paramount significance, shaping our interactions and relationships.

The concept of ‘Life is an Echo’ serves as constant reminder that our actions yield consequences that inevitably return to us, much like the seeds we sow reaping what we have sown. It underscores the notion that what we give to others ultimately finds its way back into our own lives. Hence, it is wiser to assist others, honor our elders, and show love to fellow beings, as these actions contribute to a cycle of benevolence ----an echo of our own deeds.

It is crucial to remember that the concept of ‘Life is an Echo’ can be interpreted and articulated in diverse ways, contingent on individual beliefs and personal experiences. The central message remains consistent : our actions and choices bear consequences that resonate back into our lives.

List of Narratives

1. Our Actions , our reflections

The phrase "Our actions, our reflection" encapsulates the idea that our choices and behavior in life serve as a clear mirror reflecting our unique identities. It implies that our actions act as a transparent window through which our character, values, and beliefs are visible, both to ourselves and to those around us. Essentially, this expression underscores the concept that our outward conduct directly mirrors our inner state.

For instance, consider a scenario where our financial needs drive us to act selfishly, causing harm to another person. In such a case, our decision to exploit and opportunity for financial gain by deceiving someone in need reflects greed and an unethical approach. Conversely, a person of integrity might willingly forego personal gains to assist a stranger in need, demonstrate compassion and selflessness.

Now, let's delve into the story of a skilled motor mechanic who navigates the intricate web of interconnectedness in life and the profound consequences that shape his existence. It is often observed that individuals in humble circumstances, such as the mechanic in our story, continually struggle to provide a decent life for his family. Paradoxically, his poverty often arises from their unwavering commitments to honesty, while dishonest individuals may amass wealth rapidly.

Here is a story of a motor mechanic Roky

Roky epitomizes unwavering character, embodying the highest moral values of humanity. Now, let's dive into his remarkable story.

Rocky, a skilled motor mechanic with years of dedication to a service center, faced a profound moral dilemma. His manager, Mr. Jokey, had developed an unsettling habit of engaging in unethical business practices. When faced with situations where customers' vehicles required minor repairs, such as refilling gas in air conditioners, Mr. Jokey insisted issuing a bill for complete air conditioners replacement, which cost a staggering Rs.25,000. In reality, the only necessary action was a relatively inexpensive gas refill, costing a mere Rs. 2000/- This disparity allowed Mr. Jokey to embezzle a substantial amount of money, all while escaping the notice of the service center's owner.

In the face of such dishonesty and deceit, Mr. Rocky unwaveringly refused to be complicit in these fraudulent activities. His commitment to honesty and ethical conduct ultimately, led to his dismissal from the service center.

Despite his humble financial circumstances, Rokey was a man of unwavering integrity and honesty, diligently supporting his family with his meagre income. However, the unpredictability of life brought unexpected challenges. His world turned upside down when his wife fell seriously ill, requiring urgent medical attention. With limited savings, he struggled to afford the costly treatment she needed, leading him to seek help from a local clinic.

In pursuit of immediate income, he made the courageous decision to establish a makeshift roadside workshop, equipped with modest tools. His dedication and sincerity translated into meager daily earnings, but times were tough. Financial constraints prevented him from purchasing the expensive medications his wife needed, and her condition worsened.

Determined to earn extra money, he resolved to work tirelessly the following day, hoping to secure additional funds for his ailing spouse. Unfortunately, fate dealt him a cruel hand. Torrential downpours persisted throughout the day, making it nearly impossible for potential customers to approach his workshop. Desperate to secure the necessary funds for his wife's medical care , he stood ready to expend every ounce of effort, labor, and skill to ensure no customer left unattended.

Despite his unwavering determination, the heavy rain left the broad highway, where he had set up his workshop, completely deserted. His heart raced with anxiety as everything seemed to conspire against his wishes. He anxiously waited throughout the day, fervently praying for a miracle to bring him customers. As evening descended and his prayers went unanswered, he gradually lost hope. With a heavy heart, he closed his workshop and trudged wearily back home.

He was eager to reach home as soon as possible, but the daunting challenge of acquiring essential medicines weighed heavily on his mind. His legs quivered, struggling to maintain their pace. After covering only a short distance, he spotted and elegant lady stranded by the roadside, her high-end car parked nearby. She appeared fatigued and disheartened, likely in need of assistance. Rocky's heart brimmed with hope. Here was a potential customer who might offer generous compensation if he could repair the car under the dim, stormy skies. He hastened his steps and arrived at her vehicle.

As an unfamiliar, poorly dressed man approached her rapidly, the lady was filled with apprehension. Recent news of highway robberies during odd hours flashed through her mind. Could this disheveled stranger be another threat? Rocky attempted to convey warmth with a reassuring smile, but the lady's anxiety lingered. She had attempted to flag down passing motorists for help over the past few hours, to no avail. Was he plotting to rob her ? The shabbily dressed man did not inspire confidence; he appeared impoverished and famished. Rocky empathized with an elegant lady, who stood vulnerable amid stormy downpour. He sensed her profound fear, stemming from her isolation and the breakdown of her car in the adverse circumstances.

"Respected madam', Rocky kindly addressed her, " I have come to offer my assistance. Why don't you stay inside the car where it's dry and warm ? By the way, my name is Rocky, and I'm a motor mechanic. I am here to help passengers in distress, Now, all you seem to have is a flat tire, but I understand it can be quite an issue, especially for someone in your position."

Without waiting for her response, Rocky promptly slid beneath the car, searching for a suitable spot to position the jack. After some efforts, he successfully raised the car. Soon, he accessed the spare tire from the trunk and proceeded to change it. The ground beneath was soaked with mud, and Rocky couldn't help but get dirty in the process. As he tightened the lug nuts, the lady rolled down her car window and struck up a conversation. She introduced herself as a traveler from, St. Albans, UK, passing through. Despite her bewilderment at the unusual situation, she couldn't express enough gratitude for his timely help.

Rocky merely smiled as he closed the trunk. The elegant lady inquired about the amount she owed him, willing to pay any sum in appreciation of his assistance. Rocky was indeed in need of money, but he paused for a moment to reflect. He realized that the lady wasn't a customer but rather someone vulnerable in need of help. Helping another person transcended mere monetary transactions; it was a fundamental act of humanity. Rockey believed that the true service was about aiding those in need without expecting anything in return. He considered it an opportunity to be of service to his fellow human beings, trusting that such acts of kindness would be rewarded in unexpected ways.

With a sincere tone, Rocky replied, " madam, if you truly wish to repay me, the next time you encounter someone in need, extend your help to them as I have to you today. That, for me, would be payment enough. I will receive my reward if you remember this gesture." He waited until the lady started her car and drove away, content in the knowledge that he had made a difference in her day.

Despite disheartening day, he found solace on his way home, albeit briefly. The fleeting contentment was eclipsed by the pressing need for money to purchase essential medication. His heart yearned to help the woman in need, but his conscience reminded him of past mistakes. Nonetheless, this presented an opportunity to gather the funds needed for his ailing wife's health. He felt a surge of pride for prioritizing humanity over personal gain, in stark contrast to the world's wealthiest individuals who often pursue more wealth relentlessly, neglecting their duty to help others, He earnestly prayed for divine intervention to assist his ailing wife,.

The woman. Overwhelmed with gratitude, believed that a benevolent soul had come to her rescue in her dire circumstances. Had it not been for Rocky's timely assistance, unimaginable misfortune might have befallen her. Stranded on the roadside for what seemed like an eternity, she trembled with fear, her thoughts consumed by the hope of divine intervention. Now, her agony was alleviated, and hunger gnawed at her insides as she hadn't eaten since morning.

Several miles down the road, she stumbled upon a modest eatery, prompting her to seek nourishment and respite before continuing her journey home. The establishment had a dull, uninviting exterior, surrounded by small huts housing working-class patrons. It felt alien to her, a place seemingly beneath her social status. Yet. hunger showed no discrimination, and her stomach's relentless protests demanded immediate sustenance, regardless of her station in life. Hungry and with no one , regardless of their wealth, able to provide anything other than food --- be it of high or low quality --- she reluctantly entered the restaurant, driven solely by her overpowering hunger. She occupied a vacant corner seat and waited for a waiter.

A teenager, approximately 15 years old, approached her table to take her order. Upon seeing the lady soaked from head to toe, with water cascading from her hair, he promptly procured a fresh towel and directed her to the nearest restroom. As she dried herself with the clean towel, a sense of relief washed over her. This young boy, the restaurant's youngest waiter, continued to wait on her with an infectious smile.

Throughout the day, the young boy had tirelessly served customers, never allowing the demands of his job to diminish his cheerful demeanor. The elegant lady couldn't help but notice his slight limp and signs of discomfort, yet he remained unwavering in his commitment to providing excellent service. She marveled at how someone with so little could exhibit such selfless generosity towards a stranger, reminding her of Rocky's kindness.

Being in a place she didn't particularly fancy and trying out unfamiliar cuisine, the lady found solace in the precious moments of genuine human kindness. She discovered that those who lacked financial wealth or material comforts often possessed a richer humanity compared to those who were affluent but lacked a touch of empathy.

Upon finishing her meal, the lady handed the young boy a crips one-hundred-pound sterling note as payment. The boy hurried to fetch her change, expecting a gratuity for his service. However, to his surprise, when he returned, the lady had vanished without a trace. Puzled and concerned, he set off on a quest to locate her.

Failing to find any trace of her, he reluctantly resumed his duties, clearing the table for new patrons. Then a small piece of paper attached to a business card caught his eye. The note read: " You need not concern yourself with the change money; you owe me nothing. Before coming here, someone extended his kindness to me with a smile and taught me a valuable lesson about helping others in need. I am passing that kindness on to you. If you wish to repay me, continue this chain of aiding those less fortunate. Perhaps, in the end, your kindness will be repaid by a higher power. "Beneath the napkin, he discovered five more one-hundred bills.

From that moment on, the boy found it difficult to concentrate on his duties. His mind was preoccupied with thoughts on the mysterious lady, the money, and the heartfelt message she had left. How could she have known the dire financial situation his family was facing ? His mother was battling a severe illness, and his father, Mr. Rocky, had recently lost his job.

He knew the weight of his father's worries. Throughout his life, Mr. Rocky had worked tirelessly as an auto mechanic to provide for his family,. It was late at night, and his father was fast asleep. Gently placing five one-hundred-pound bills near his pillow, he whispered softly, " Everything is going to be alright."

Mr. Rocky awoke to find the unexpected windfall and was overwhelmed with joy. He had initially declined the elegant lady's offer of financial help, and now, it seemed, a generous providence had blessed him. In that moment, Rock recalled an age-old saying: " We are often taught to treat others as we wish to be treated. What goes around comes around. Sooner or later our actions are rewarded or punished in kind. Good deeds yield good results, and vice-versa."

2. Virtue of Honesty.

This tale revolves around the life of Mr. Harry, an exceptionally honest officer. Despite working amidst dubious and dishonest colleagues, he frequently found himself the target of ridicule. Harry led a modest life , and people often laughed at his simple attire, his ordinary wristwatch, his old fashioned spectacles, and everything else about him. Undeterred by the hostility and aggression directed towards him , Harry remained content with his commitment to honesty and his unassuming existence. His greatest love was reserved for his only son, Rakesh.

Harry's wife, Sudha, was a devoted homemaker with a strong religious disposition, wholly dedicated to her family. Together, they lived a joyous life. Rakesh a brilliant 10th grade student enrolled in a prestigious school, was well aware of his fathers' unwavering principles. Regardless of the circumstances, Harry remained steadfast in his commitment to honesty. In the office, he endured the mockery of his colleagues, refusing to indulge in extravagant spending on fashionable attire, unlike his peers. He commuted on his old scooter or relied on public transportation.

Rakesh followed in his father's footsteps. As a diligent student, teachers praised him, but his classmates kept their distance , mocking his simplicity. Just like his father, Rakesh was the subject of ridicule among many students. He pedaled to school on his aging bicycle, while his peers arrived in bikes and cars. Other students lived in lavishly furnished homes with separate rooms and full air-conditioning, a stark contrast to the modest life that Rakesh and his family embraced.

In the meanwhile , Rakesh found himself lost in contemplation about his family's living situation. Their home merely a rented space, and they had to endure their landlord's frequent scolding . The condition of their water and electricity supply were unimaginably dire. Rakesh had only one school uniform, which had become threadbare with use. When it came to pocket money, he had to wait for months, well aware that his father's colleagues were ,living opulent lives.

His father's coworkers were all financially comfortable, enjoying every luxury imaginable. Rakesh's frustration grew as he considered his father's unwavering commitment to honesty. He yearned for his father to adopt a more pragmatic approach, to earn abundantly by any means necessary, so they could also experience the pleasures enjoyed by his friends. However, his father's unyielding dedication to honesty acted as a formidable barrier to these desires.

As Rakesh wrestled with these conflicting thoughts, he returned home to a devastating sight. His father had suffered a severe and potentially fatal heart attack.

Summoning his son, he offered heartfelt advice, saying, " Follow the path of honesty, my child, and you will find tranquility in every endeavor you pursue in life. Remember, an honest person may face inconveniences, but a dishonest one is destined for log-term suffering."

Growing increasingly exasperated with his father's principles, Rakesh retorted, "Dad, it's truly unfortunate that you're leaving this world with an empty bank account. You've often criticized others as corrupt and dishonest, but those very individuals have left substantial fortune, houses, and properties for their children. Our current home is a rented apartment with dilapidated walls, a decrepit ceiling fan, and unreliable water supply in the bathrooms. My friends drive brand new cars and bikes, while I'm stuck pedaling an ancient, useless bicycle. How embarrassing ? I'm afraid I cannot adhere to your notion of honesty."

Upon hearing his son's perspective, Mr. Harry suffered another fatal attack and passed away shortly after.

Time marched on, and after completing his education, Rakesh attended an interview at a prestigious multinational corporation. During the interview, the chairman of th interview committee inquired about his father's name and address.

Rakesh responded, " Sir, I am Rakesh, the son of late Mr. harry, the Govt. Officer.'

The chairman interjected, " Oh my goodness, you're Mr. Harry's son, the Government Officer.?" Turning to other committee members, he exclaimed, " This man, Mr. Harry, once came to my aid when my own family and acquaintances had turned their back on me. He was a stranger at the time, but as a Government Officer, he verified my credentials and vouched for me. Thanks to his verification and recommendation, I am where I am today. He did it without any personal gain, without even knowing me . He did it solely to assist a candidate in need." Addressing Rakesh, he added, " I have no further questions for you. Consider yourself selected for this job. Ome tomorrow to collect your letter of appointment.' Stunned and disoriented by the Chairman's unexpected response, Rakesh left the interview in a state of disbelief.'

In the final outcome, Rakesh emerged as the Corporate Affairs manager of the company, enjoying a company car, a personal chauffeur, a well furnished residence, and a monthly salary of Rs. 50,000/- along with various additional benefits and travel privileges. The Company's Head Quarter was located in the UK, necessitating periodic visits. Rakesh dedicated himself tirelessly to achieve commendable results for the Company. After five years of dedicated service, an unexpected proposition came his way. A prominent business tycoon offered him an enticing job in his industrial Estate, contingent on Rakesh sharing confidential company information. To sweeten the deal, an unimaginable cash reward was promised, Rakesh's ego swelled momentarily as he contemplated the allure of career advancement and substantial financial gain.

However, a moral dilemma soon gnawed at him. He had diligently and honestly toiled for the past five years, earning the respect and admiration of his colleagues. Could he betray their trust and compromise his hard-earned reputation? Ultimately , he resolved to decline the proposal, valuing integrity over monetary gain.

A year later, during the company's Annual general meeting, the Managing Director announced his intention to resign and sought a successor known for unwavering integrity. A thorough search led to a list of five potential candidates, which was subsequently narrowed down through interviews. Rakesh received a call to appear before the interview board at the company's headquarters.

During the interview, he was asked about the secret to his success. Tears welled up in his eyes as he responded, " My father paved the path for my success. It was only after his passing that I realized he may have been financially modest, but he was immensely rich in integrity, discipline, and honesty.

The Chairman inquired about his tears, reminding him that he was no more a child to grieve his father's memory so deeply. Rakesh pleaded, " please do not ask me such questions, they pain me.' The Chairman recognizing Rakesh's honesty, asked why such a question hurt hm.

Rakesh explained, " It pains me because, at the time of my father's death, I insulted him for being an honest man of integrity. I hope he can forgive me now. When I entered the first interview, I had little faith in my abilities, and was selected solely based on my father's honesty and integrity. All credit goes to him.

Finally, the Chairman asked, "Will you continue to follow your father's last advice of honesty ?

Rakesh fell into prolonged silence, struggling to respond. He remembered his late father's plea for forgiveness and admitted, " I now hold my father in the highest regard. I have placed is picture next to the image of God in my home. My current position is a testament to the wisdom of his words and my earlier folly. I revere him above all else and shall never forget his advice.'

The Chairman commended Rakesh, revealing that the offer of the Industrial Estate and cash reward had been a test of his integrity, devised by the organization. Rekesh had passed with flying color.

In the end, Rakesh had embraced his father's values of honesty and integrity. He realized that honesty, though slow to yield rewards, eventually builds a lasting reputation, integrity, discipline, and self-control, he learned, were the true sources of wealth, transcending mere financial success. As he reflected on his journey, Rakesh and his colleagues took pride in their unwavering commitment to honesty, knowing that no legacy is as enriching as that of integrity. Despite occasional challenges, they remained steadfast in their dedication to truthfulness, cherishing the virtue of honesty above all else.

In the ultimate outcome, Rakesh ascended to the position of Corporate Affair Manager within the company. This role brought with it a company car, a personal chauffeur, a well-appointed residence , and a monthly salary of Rs.50,000/-, accompanied by numerous additional benefits and travel privileges. The company's headquarters were situated in the UK, requiring periodic visits. Rakesh wholeheartedly dedicated himself to achieving commendable results for the company over the course of years.

However, an unexpected position came his way after this dedicated service. A prominent business tycoon offered him an enticing job within his industrial estate, contingent upon Rakesh sharing confidential company information. To sweeten the deal, an unimaginable cash award was promised. Rakesh's ego briefly swelled as he contemplated the allure of career advancement and substantial financial gain.

Nevertheless, a moral dilemma soon began to gnaw at him. He had diligently and honestly toiled for the past five years, earning respect and admiration of his colleagues. Could he betray their trust and compromise his hard-earned reputation ? Ultimately, he resolved to decline the proposal, valuing integrity over monetary gain.

A year later, during the company's Annual general Meeting, The Managing Director announced his intention to resign and sought a successor known for unwavering integrity. A thorough search led to a list of five potential candidates, which was subsequently narrowed down through interviews. Rakesh received a call to appear before the interview board at the company's headquarters.

During the interview, he was asked about the secret to his success. Tears welled up in his eyes as he responded,

" My father paved the path for my success. It was only after his passing that I realized he may have been financially modest, but he was immensely rich in integrity, discipline, and honesty."

The Chairman inquired about his tears, reminding him that he was no longer a child to grieve his father's memory so deeply. Rakesh pleaded, "Please do not ask me such questions, they pain me. " The Chairman , recognizing Rakesh's honesty, asked why such a question hurts him.

Rakesh explained, " It pains me because, at the time of my father's death, I insulted him for being an honest man of integrity. I hope he can forgive me now. When I entered the first interview, I had little faith in my abilities and was selected solely based on my father's honesty and integrity. All credit goes to him.

Finally, the Chairman asked, " Will you continue to follow your father's last advice of honesty ? Rakesh fell into prolonged silence, struggling to respond. He remembered his late father's plea for forgiveness and admitted, " I now hold my father in the highest regard. I have placed his picture next to the image of God at my home. My current position is a testament to the wisdom of his words and my earlier folly. I revere him above all else and shall never forget his advice."

The Chairman commended Rakesh, revealing that the offer of the Industrial Estate and cash reward had been a test of his integrity, devised by the organization. Rakesh had passed with flying colors.

In the end, Rakesh had embraced his father's values of honesty and integrity. He realized that honesty, though slow to yield rewards, eventually builds a lasting reputation. Integrity, discipline, and self-control, he learned , were the true sources of wealth, transcending mere financial success. As he reflected on his journey, Rakesh and his colleagues took pride in their unwavering commitment to honesty, knowing that no legacy is as enriching as that of integrity. Despite occasional challenges, they remained steadfast in their dedication to truthfulness, cherishing the virtue of honesty above all else.

3.The Power of Diligence

How small actions make a big difference.

I am Ankit, and at the age of 20, I find myself amidst a myriad of challenges, encompassing both financial and non-financial aspects, while residing in a middle-class household, My father, a small shopkeeper, earns a modest income, and my mother, a devoted homemaker with strong religious beliefs, diligently manages our household on a limited budget, striving to save wherever possible. My parents exercise strict financial vigilance, closely monitoring the spending habits of all family members.

Observing my parents' hardship, I am resolute in my determination to improve our family's financial position. I actively search for a job opportunities and devote my time to my studies in pursuit of this goal. As the scorching summer sun beats down, I prepare for a crucial job interview, burning the midnight oil. Yet, my efforts face obstacles, not only from the oppressive heat but also from my father's concerns about the electricity bill. My late-night studying becomes a source of irritation for him, leading to frequent reminders to turn off the lights. In the morning , my mother engages in monologues, seemingly oblivious to others' needs, adding to my frustration. The stringent household rules, covering everything from frugality to waste avoidance, weigh heavily on me.

While I acknowledge my parents kind hearts, their preoccupation with my sister's marriage, given her age of over 30, adds to their financial burden. Each marriage proposal comes with an expensive list of expensive demands. To meet the minimum requirements for her wedding, we estimate needing ten lakh rupees. This ongoing concern has made my parents more frugal, traditional, and possessive. I have personally committed to assisting them in this endeavor.

On the day of my crucial job interview, I hurriedly prepared to ensure punctuality. At home, I thought, " If succeed today, I will take responsibility for my sister's wedding. My parents endure immense social pressure due to its delay. Once I secure the job, I will spare no efforts to bring happiness to my sister and parents, putting an end to the daily conflicts and arguments in our household, from early morning quarrels to late-night disputes. These disturbances cast a shadow over every step I take at home."

Every morning, I am greeted by a barrage of demands. As soon as I wake up. My father's voice instructs me to fold my bed and store it in the storeroom. In the bathroom, I am compelled to bathe in the darkness as per my father's decree. Emerging from the shower, my mother promptly reminds me to put the towel in its designated place, lest it be discarded. It's an overwhelming start to the day, a daily ritual that repeats unfailingly. In essence, they keep me on my toes, following their directives.

Just before leaving the house, the litany of instructions continues, including reminders to turn off the fan, retrieve my slippers from the bathroom , deposit my used clothes in the laundry basket, clean my dirty shoes, and button up my shirt. These minor infractions are pointed out as if I were a child and a habitual offender.

I fervently pray to the heavens, “Please grant me a job interview, “and then I make my escape. Frustrated by the stringent rules governing my every move under my parents’ watchful eyes, T yearn for an opportunity to break free and find employment.

The day of my interview finally arrives, but it comes with its own set of challenges. The interview is scheduled for 10 AM, but as I glance at the office veranda, I notice that many bulbs are still lit, waiting to be switched off. Remembering my father’s advice, I set my bag aside and diligently turned off all unnecessary lights, as daylight requires no extra illumination. In the process, my hands get smeared with grime from the electricity board, and I decide to wash them in the bathroom. However, the tap is carelessly left open, and water is steadily dripping away. It is a blatant waste of this precious resource, reminding me of my mother’s scolding as I tighten the tap to conserve water. Returning to my place, I glance around to ensure no other candidates are present. To my surprise, they have all disappeared. Puzzled, I spot a notice on the board: “Interviews scheduled on the second floor.” I grab my bag and ascend to the second floor, eager to face the challenges that lie ahead.

“What in the world is this” ? I whispered to myself upon spotting spilled water on the staircase. It was a hazardous situation, as someone could easily slip and sustain a serious injury. Recognizing the need for action, I scoured the area for cleaning material, but none were in sight. Making a quick decision, I headed to the nearby trash bin, retrieved some discarded papers, and began to dry the stairs. It became apparent that carelessness was a recurring theme in this office, where no one seemed to take responsibility for anything.

Upon reaching the second floor, I discovered that interviews were already in progress. Candidates were being ushered in and out at an astonishing speed. I couldn't comprehend how through evaluations could be conducted in such a short time. Each candidate had a file filled with credentials, but it appeared that these files were only briefly glanced at before being returned without a detailed examination.

When it was finally my turn, I placed my profile in front of the interview board and braced myself for the expected tough questions. However, to my surprise, the Chairman didn't open my file. Instead, he fixed his gaze on my face, creating an unsettling moment that filled me with anxiety, anticipating some sort of problem.

After scrutinizing my face for a moment, he abruptly asked, " When are you joining ?" This question caught me off guard, as no other inquiries were made, and my credentials remained untouched. His words made me feel as if I were the subject of a joke, but he reassured me that it was a fact, not a jest.

No further questions were posed, no documents were reviewed. The Chairman explained that they had been closely observing all the candidates from the moment they entered the office premises, monitoring everyone via CCTV cameras. Whie every candidate had come and gone, none had bothered to turn off lights, close running taps, or address the wet stairs. I, on the other hand, had taken the initiative to attend to these small but significant details that mattered most in life.

The Chairman continued, inquiring whether this attentiveness was a personal hobby or if I had received specific training for it. I replied." No, Sir, I learned to do this out of necessity,' Perplexed he pressed further, " What do you mean by necessity? " What compelled you to do so?

I explained, "Sir, the credit for my attention to such details goes to my parents, who constantly guided me in this regard. I must admit, however, that I used to perceive their advice as a mere annoyance and considered it a bad habit of theirs. I mistakenly thought they were being harsh and doing it to trouble me."

The Chairman responded warmly, " Your parents are truly blessed for instilling in you the understanding of life's value.'

I could not bear my guilt any longer, I had misunderstood my parents all along. Every time they had advised me to pay attention to the little things , I had perceived it as hostility. They were fulfilling their duty as loving perfect parents. In our lives, we often become indignant at our parents' rightful and well-intentioned reprimands, forgetting that they re our greatest well-wishers who desire nothing but the best for us.

That day, I made a solemn commitment to listen to my parents' advice and follow it wholeheartedly. I felt a profound sense of happiness and pride in my parents. Upon returning home, I embraced my mother and father, apologized for my previous defiance, and expressed my gratitude to them.

Now , I understand that parental guidance transcended any academic qualifications in the world.

4 The Test of Character

Atop a picturesque hill, nestled in a charming village, dwelled a close-knit community defined by their unwavering work ethic, sincerity, and innate simplicity. Predominately farmers, these villagers routinely ventured to bustling cities to trade their abundant harvests. At the center of their settlement stood a revered shrine, an unspoken testament to their devotion. This sacred place held immense historical significance, although its construction lacked any documented record. Its architectural splendor, evident in its unique layout and style, captivated all who beheld it.

Within this sanctuary, an idol stood, its crown adorned with a precious diamond of unparalleled beauty. The beauty of upholding the shrine' sanctity rested on the shoulders of the chief priest, a meticulous guardian. The Chief Priest, fastidious about cleanliness, assigned villagers to take turn maintaining the premises condition. On a fateful day, the responsibility of tending to the shire fell upon a young man named Mukesh, renowned throughout the village for his unwavering integrity and moral compass. Mukesh possessed an uncommon strength derived from from his unwavering commitment to righteousness, even in the face of daunting dilemma.

Dutifully, Mukesh fetched water from a nearby well and began cleansing the shrine's entire floor, adhering to tradition. However, it was strictly forbidden to use water on the idol itself. Instead, a pristine, damp cloth was required for this sacred task. As Mukesh delicately wiped the deity's visage, a sudden realization struck him – the precious diamond nestled within the idol's crown had vanished without a trace. He scoured every nook and cranny of the shrine in vain, desperately searching for the missing gem,

The following day, news of the stolen diamond spread rapidly, casting a shadow of despair over the village. This cherished possession, believed to bring prosperity and good fortune to the villagers, was now gone. Suspicion hung thick in the air, and all eyes turned to Mukesh. To his fellow villagers, he now appeared to be the prime suspect in this unsettling mystery.

Mukesh did not flee the village but stood his ground, vehemently asserting his innocence regarding the missing diamond. He made it unequivocally clear that when he last tended to the shrine, the diamond had been securely in the idol's crown. However, his protestations fell on deaf ears, and the cloud of suspicion continued to envelop him. Mukesh's integrity was on the line, compelling him to take matters into his own hands and uncover the true culprit.

Driven by an unyielding sense of duty, Mukesh embarked on an unrelenting quest to unravel the mystery of the stolen diamond. Initially, his focus was on the chief priest's servant, who had convenient access to the shrine. After days of investigation, Mukesh conducted that the servant was innocent, as he had never ventured near the deity's idol.

Undaunted, Mukesh redirected his attention to various villagers who frequented the shrine. Yet, this too proved fruitless, as the villagers held the shrine in the highest regard, making them unlikely suspects.

With each passing day, Mukesh found himself in a precarious position. He devoted countless hours to probing the incident, engaging in conversations with villagers, and scouring for any elusive clues that could lead him to the thief. Balancing this relentless pursuit with his daily livelihood was no easy task. As days turned into weeks and weeks into months, Mukesh's determination remained unwavering. Despite encountering setbacks and apparent deed ends, he steadfastly remained committed to uncovering the truth.

One evening, while Mukesh was in deep contemplation near the village pond, he noticed a glimmer of light emanating from beneath the water's surface. His curiosity piqued, he leaned in closer, discovering a hidden diamond among the pond's reeds. This was no ordinary stone; it was a precious gem that sparkled brilliantly.

The allure of the diamond's value was evident to Mukesh. Thoughts of the riches it could bring, the admiration he might receive, tempted him. However, Mukesh was not just any villager; he had imbibed the village's values of honesty and integrity since childhood. Additionally, he had spent years in the selfless service of the chief priest, learning the importance of moral conduct.

The prospect of overnight wealth clashed with Mukesh's principles, creating a profound internal conflict. One side of his mind whispered seductively, urging him to keep the diamond hidden. Meanwhile, his conscience, guided by the teachings of honesty and selflessness, reminded him of his responsibility to restore the diamond to its rightful place, the temple.

Days turned into nights, and Mukesh found no peace. His troubled countenance became evident to those who knew him well. Friends and family observed his restlessness, sensing the inner turmoil that engulfed his soul.

Amidst this struggle, one evening, as the sun painted the sky with hues of crimson, Mukesh reached a turning point. He resolved to bring the stolen gem back to the temple, aiming to restore its sanctity. The village seemed to exhale a collective sigh of relief, even without knowing the cause, as if sensing the imminent return of harmony.

Entering the hallowed precincts of the temple, Mukesh found solace in the serenity that enveloped the sacred space. With steady steps, he approached the priest, whose eyes widened with a mix of surprise and gratitude as Mukesh presented the long-lost diamond.

The temple, once tarnished by the theft, now basked in renewed glory. The worshippers, unaware of Mukesh's selfless act, experienced a sense of spiritual fulfillment that surpassed the mere return of a stolen gem.

Word of Mukesh's choice eventually spread throughout the village. Admiration for his integrity and rectitude surged through the community like wildfire. His act of moral strength became a legend, an inspiration for those faced with similar choices.

Mukesh's inner turmoil had been replaced by a profound sense of peace. The weight of his conscience had been lifted, leaving behind a spirit unburdened and filled with purpose. From that day forth, he became an emblem of moral strength, a guiding light for those navigating ethical dilemmas.

Mukesh's tale spread far and wide, not just within the village but beyond its borders. It became a timeless reminder that true character is tested in the crucible of moral dilemmas. And when one listens to the call of their inner conscience, it leads to a path illuminated by righteousness and virtue. His story was retold for generations, inspiring individuals to choose the path of integrity and moral rectitude, emphasizing the profound impact of a single act of unwavering honesty.

5 The Ripple Effect

In a vibrant metropolis teeming with people in a constant rush, there resided a young woman by the name Kusum. Amidst the relentless commotion enveloping her, Kusum harbored a heart brimming with kindness of compassion. She firmly believed in transformative potential of small acts of benevolence, recognizing their ability to set forth far-reaching ripples of positivity.

On a bright and cheerful morning, as Kusum embarked on her journey to work, her discerning eye caught sight of an elderly gentleman grappling with the weight of a burdened bag of groceries. Without hesitation, she hurried over to extend her helping hand. The elderly man, appreciative of her gesture, graciously accepted, and together they made their way to his modest apartment.

During the brief traverse, the man, known as Mr. Mahinder, imparted fragments of his life's narrative to Kusum. His twilight years had been marked by formidable trials and an overwhelming sense of solitude. Kusum's unfeigned empathy and eagerness to assist had profoundly touched his heart.

Galvanized by their encounter, Kusum resolved to bring about a positive change in Mr. Mahinder's life. She initiated regular visits, offering homemade meals and engaging in heartfelt conversations. In the process, she unearthed Mr. Mahinder's dormant talent as a painter, which had long been eclipsed by the circumstances he faced.

Fueled by her deep compassion, Kusum spurred Mr. Mahinder to reclaim his paintbrush. She orchestrated and art exhibition in his honor, extending invitations to the local community to marvel at his artistic prowess. The event proved to be as astounding triumph, with Mr. Mahender's paintings swiftly disappearing into eager hands within a matter of days.

The tale of Kusum's benevolence and Mr. Mahinder's extraordinary talent reverberated throughout the city, touching the hearts of individuals from all walks of life. It became the catalyst for an outpouring of kindness. One after another, the city's inhabitants stepped forward to lend aid to those in need, igniting a cascade of compassion.

Shopkeepers began donating surplus food to homeless shelters, strangers generously devoted their time to volunteer at local charitable organizations , and children enthusiastically orchestrated fund raisers to support causes close to their hearts. The reverberations of Kusum's initial act of kindness gained momentum with each passing day.

News of the city's remarkable transformation reached far and wide, drawing visitors from neighboring towns and cities who sought to witness the enchantment that kindness had woven. They departed inspired, carrying the torch of compassion back to their own communities, thereby extending, carrying the torch of compassion back to their own communities, thereby extending the ripple effect even further.

Kusum, the young woman who had simply wanted to make a difference in one person's life now found herself at the center of a movement. She became a symbol of kindness and compassion, reminding people that even the smallest acts could have immeasurable impact.

6. Lessons in Perseverance

In a picturesque village nested at the base of a majestic mountain, there lived a young girl named maya, celebrated for her fiery spirit and unyielding determination. She firmly believed that every challenge held the potential for growth and learning, and she welcomed them with open arms.

One fateful day, news spread throughout the village about a prestigious writing competition in the nearby city. This competition offered the promise of recognition and elusive chance to be published - a dream of great significance for aspiring writers like Maya. Filled with excitement , Maya embarked on a journey to pour her heart and souls into crafting the perfect story for submission

Weeks turned into months as Maya became fully immersed in her writing, meticulously refining every word and nuance. Finally, the day arrived to submit her entry. With trembling hands, she carefully sealed the envelope, releasing her manuscript into the unknown, filled with hope and anticipation.

Days turned into weeks, and weeks into months, yet maya received no word about the competition. Doubt began to creep into her thoughts, suggesting that perhaps it was time to give up. However, Maya's unwavering determination continued to burn within her, urging her to persist.

Undaunted, maya pressed on with her writing, exploring new genres and styles. She actively sought feedback from fellow writers, dedicating herself tirelessly to honing her craft. The rejections she encountered only fueled her determination to achieve success.

Then, on an ordinary day while strolling through the village square, Maya received an unexpected letter--- an invitation to a writing workshop hosted by a renowned author. In that moment, Maya's heart skipped a beat as she realized that her arduous efforts had not gone unnoticed.

The workshop marked a profound turning point in Maya's journey. Surrounded by fellow writers and guided by a seasoned mentor, she absorbed invaluable lessons in persistence and the craft writing. The workshop reignited the flames of her passion and restored her unwavering belief in her own capabilities.

Armed with newfound confidence, Maya returned to her writing with a fresh zeal. She submitted her work to numerous publications and entered multiple competitions. Each rejection, instead of disheartening her, became a stepping stone, imparting vital lessons in resilience and the importance of never giving up.

Then came that pivotal day when maya received an email that would forever change the course of her life. It was an acceptance letter from a prestigious publishing house, expressing not only an interest in publishing one of her stories but also offering a book deal—a dream come true.

Maya's unyielding determination had finally borne fruit. Her journey, filled with challenges and setbacks, had culminated in this triumphant moment. She had conquered self-doubt, defied rejection, and overcome countless obstacles, emerging as a writer stronger and more resilient than ever before.

Maya's story resonated far and wide, inspiring budding writers everywhere. She became a beacon of hope and a living testament to the power of unwavering perseverance. People from all walks of life drew strength from her journey, reminding themselves that challenges were not barriers but rather opportunities for personal growth.

Thus, the chronicle of Maya and her lessons in persistence echoed across generations –a timeless reminder that the determination , even in the face of adversity, had the power to turn dreams into reality. Maya's narrative became a guiding star for those who dared to chase their passions, instilling in them the conviction that with unwavering resolve, they too could overcome and obstacle that crossed their path.

7. WHO IS RICHER THAN A RICH MAN.?

“Don’t make more money, make more friends. “

(Story of Bill Gates)

Soham, a 10th-grade student from a humble background, often found himself lost in daydreams of a life where his parents were affluent, affording him the privileges that came with wealth. In his imagination, wealth equated to the freedom to pursue one’s passions without the shackles of financial worries, be it a fulfilling career without concern for the paychecks or indulging in interests without the need to earn a livelihood from them. This vision inspired Soham to set his sights on prosperity, leading him to embark on a quest to gain knowledge about wealthy individuals.

During his journey, Soham’s exploration brought him to the revelation that Mr. Bill Gates held the title of the world’s richest person. Soham devoted his full attention to uncovering the life story of this celebrated figure. . As he delved into Bill gates’ biography, he learned that Gates was born into a privileged family on October 28,1955. His father was a lawyer, and his grandfather had served as the President of the National Bank. Gates, from an early age, exhibited a fervent passion for computers and nurtured ambitions’ of becoming a millionaire by establishing his own company.

Fueled by his unwavering love for computers, Gates crossed paths with kindred spirit named Paul Allen.

Together, they ventured into the business world after their studies. Despite facing numerous initial challenges, they founded a software company known as Microsoft in 1975. The pivotal moment arrived in 1986, after 11 years of relentless efforts, when Bill Gates introduced the revolutionary software Windows. Guided by a grand vision and an unyielding work ethic, Bill Gates propelled Microsoft to the summit of the software industry, ultimately becoming the world's wealthiest individual.

Bill Gates' name graced the top of Forbes" annual list of the world's billionaires a remarkable 16 times. He emerged as an extraordinary individual who crafted a software empire, ascending to the rank of the word's richest man.

Soham's excitement soared as he immersed himself in his biography, driven by his profound love for computers. He embarked on the captivating journey through Bill gates' life story, immersing himself in the myriad intricate details documented by various authors. Amid this exploration, he stumbled upon a particularly fascinating anecdote.

Many years ago, Bill Gates faced the brink dismissal due to the dispute with management. This pivotal moment prompted him to reconnect with long-lost friends, and their joy at then chance to sit in close proximity to the world's wealthiest man was palpable. Fueled by curiosity, one of his friends ventured to ask, "Is there anyone richer than you ?

After a thoughtful pause, Bill gates replied, “ yes , there is one individual who surpasses my wealth.” The subsequent question was swift, “ Who is this person ? ”

Bill Gates struggled to recall the man’s name but vividly remembered the circumstances. He recounted a visit to New York Airport where he had contemplated buying a newspaper from the vendor. However, a lack of small change in his pocket left him disheartened. As he prepared to walk away, the vendor noticed his dejected demeanor. Recognizing Bill gate’s earnest desire for the newspaper, the vendor kindly intervened, offering it as a gift. Bill Gates recounted this touching encounter, remembering the young boy’s face as he extended the coveted newspaper.

Caught in a perplexed predicament, I found myself hesitating to accept his generous offer, primarily due to a lack of change money, even though my eagerness to read the newspaper was undeniable. My emotions were a mix of disappointment; I couldn’t buy the paper, yet I didn’t want to decline the kind gesture. I remained silently observing the young boy, unable to make a decision. The internal struggle intensified - should I accept or decline? The temptation of the newspaper was irresistible, but my empty pockets rendered acceptance impossible. With a heavy heart, I finally uttered.” I don’t have any change money.’ In response, he smiled warmly and said, “No problem, it’s on the house.” Gratefully, I accepted the newspaper, thanking the kind young boy.

Bill Gates paused briefly, gauging his friends' reactions as they listened to his tale. After a moment, he continued, "You see, my days and nights are consumed by a busy schedule, leaving little time for trivial matters,. This incident slipped from my memory."

Life came full circle when I returned to the same airport three months later. As was my habit, I perused the newspapers and magazines displayed for sale, hoping to find some coins in my pocket, only to come up empty-handed once again. The same observant boy noticed my intent and, without a word, offered me the desired newspaper once more, declaring it was on the house. It was heartwarming moment, encountering such a compassionate young lad who willingly bestowed smiles upon strangers free of charge. My curiosity piqued, I couldn't help but ask the boy, 'dear friend, three months ago, you generously provided a newspaper for free, and today you do the same. Do you extend this kindness to everyone you encounter in such situation?

"No, I don't extend this offer to everyone. However, when I sense a string desire in a customer whom is willing to pay but unable to do so due to certain circumstances, I choose to share a portion of my profit with them. My intension is preventing someone from feeling disheartened simply due to a lack of a small amount of money.

The memory of this particular incident stayed with me, making me reflect on the principles and wisdom behind such actions. It involved a poor African American boy who had already been marginalized by white society. Despite his disadvantaged position, he displayed remarkable generosity by offering his merchandise for free to a well-dressed white individual who wanted to make a purchase but had no small change to pay for it.

While reading Bill Gates' biography, this particular anecdote deeply resonated with young Soham. The idea of a humble boy parting with his hard-earned money to help someone in need intrigued him and spurred his curiosity.

As the young reader delved further into the text, Bill gates, responding to the question, "Is there anyone richer than you ? shared his own story.

Nineteen years after after attaining the pinnacle of success, I felt a compelling need to locate this benevolent individual and repay his kindness. I assembled a dedicated team and instructed them to track down the young newspaper seller from the past. After a month and half of diligent research and investigation, they identified the former newspaper boy, who had now become a theater owner. Bill Gate personally went to meet him and asked, "Do you recognize me " ?

The man nodded with smile. " Of course you're the famous Bill Gates, the world's wealthiest individual."

Impressed, Bill gates remarked, " Your memory is truly remarkable , recalling the times when you generously provided me with free newspapers many years ago."

The man replied, " I have a strong memory, and I remember you quite well.'

Bill gates continued, " It's heartening to know you remember me. Let's strenghten our friendship. I'd like to make amends now."

" I intend to offer you everything you desire, " he added.

The man, however, replied, " You can't make amends for it."

Perplexed, Bill gates inquired, " Why not ? "

The man explained, Because I helped you when you were poor, and now you want to assist me when you are rich. How can you truly compensate for that ?

Bill Gates conceded, " I believe the young man may be richer than I am.'

The young man responded firmly, "One doesn't need to be wealthy to help other."

He continued with a powerful message, "We become truly rich when we enrich the lives of others.'

Some wise man has said, "Money and wealth means an element of vanity. Which means it is all empty. When you die, all measures of wealth and all possessions go to someone else. What goes with you is the legacy of good deeds and your integrity. And this is matched by the morals you have touched and created the legacy of your influence on others, and the memory of your good deeds.

We will be rich only if we make others rich

Our Ex-President APJ Abdul Kalam rightly said:

"Don't make more money, make more friends."

8. Power Can Corrupt a person, not his character

(Story of Lal Bahadur Shastri)

The famous saying, "Power Corrupts, " and its extension, "Absolute power corrupts absolutely, " emphasize the crucial role of power in the actions of political leaders. They utilize their authority to achieve various objectives, but the ways in which they wield this power can greatly differ. Some leaders use it for the betterment of their constituents, while other exploit it for personal gain. These two approaches to power are inherently contradictory. A leader can indeed employ their power ton serve the greater good while also reaping personal benefits. However, there are instances where leaders, under the guise of public welfare, manipulate their power solely for their self-interest.

Consequently, many elected leaders become intoxicated by the allure of power, using it recklessly. In their minds, the negative aspects of power often overshadow its potential for positive change. Nevertheless, there is an inspiring case of a prominent political figure who would later become the Prime Minister of India.

During a school debate, a teacher discussed the significant challenge of upholding unwavering moral principles while holding positions of authority. They explained how most individuals, once in power, succumb to the temptations of corruption. In the midst of this discussion, the teacher recounted the remarkable story of a humble man from a modest background who remained resolute in his commitment to ethical standards, even when occupying the highest office in a country where many others yielded to the corrosive influence of corruption.

The teacher went on to introduce the students to the name Lal bahadur Shastri, who would later become the Prime Minister of India. Following the passing of the first Prime Minister, Jawaharlal Nehru, India faced a leadership vacuum, leaving the nation eagerly awaiting a successor who could effectively guide the country, muck like Nehru did. Two individual emerged as strong contenders for the position; Morarji Desai and Lal Bahadur Shastri. Morarji Desai had seniority, extensive experience, exceptional abilities, and an unblemished reputation for honesty. In contrast, Lal Bahadur Shastri came from a humble background, led a modest life, and held a junior position. However, he possessed a remarkable degree of adaptability, unwavering principles, and grounded persona. Despite Morarji Desai's formidable credentials, it was Lal Bahadur Shastri's affable demeanor and principled approach that endeared him to the masses, ultimately leading to his victory over Morarji Desai. The choice proved to be a wise one, as Lal Bahadur Shastri went on went on to demonstrate the wisdom of his selection during is tenure as Prime Minister.

Lal Bahadur Shastri's early life was marked by his father, Sharda Prasad Shrivastva, a school teacher who passed away when Shastri was just two years old. His mother, Ram Dulari Devi, relocated with her children to her father Hazari Lal's home. It was in this metrnal household that Lal Bahadur Shastri imbibed essential virtues such as courage, universal love, patience, self-discipline, courtesy, and selflessness during his formative years, instilling within him a strong sense of ethics. He grew up holding high moral standards, even renouncing his original surname, "Shrivastava" in protest against the prevailing caste system. He adopted the title "Shastri" after completing his graduation at Kashi Vidyapeeth and became renowned for his ethical and moral principles.

When he assumed the role of railway minister, his mother, curious about his job, inquired. Shastri Ji chose not to disclose his ministerial position, simply stating that he worked for the Railway. On one occasion, he was invited as the chief guest at an event organized by the Railway ministry in his capacity as railway Minister. Before departing for the event, he informed his mother about it and its location. She eventually arrived at the event venue.

Due to the presence of the minister, heightened security measures were in place, with strict verification of attendees. When she reached the gate, the security officer stopped her for questioning. She explained that her son worked for the railway and that she had come to meet him. When asked for her son's name, her response was met with disbelief. How could a modestly dressed, ordinary woman be the mother of the railway minister? Suspicion arose in the security officer's mind, suspecting that she might be lying.

The security officer found himself in dilemma. If he allowed her entry and she turned out to be deceptive, he risked losing his post. On the other hand, if he refused her entry and she was indeed the minister's mother, he would also risk his job. Consequently, he decided to inform the minister about the situation.

A senior security officer approached Lal Bahadur Shastri and informed him that a woman was standing at the gate, claiming to be your mother and insisting on meeting you. Unable to see her due to the crowded venue, Shastri decided to personally verify her identity. Upon seeing his mother at the gate, he humbly touched her feet, brought her inside, and offered her a comfortable seat beside him. He publicly acknowledged his mother's love for him, expressing admiration for her determination in reaching the event alone.

Although it was time for him to deliver the inaugural speech, Shastri chose to remain silent and spent time talking with his mother. After a while he escorted his mother back home. Following the conclusion of the event, a press conference was held with Lal Bahadur Shastri.

The first question from a prominent journalist was surprising, "Sir, you mother was present with you. Why did you avoid addressing the public in her presence? Shastri responded candidly, "Please do not be curious. I have nothing to hide from you. I refrained from delivering my speech in her presence because I had lied to her. I hadn't informed her that I am the railway minister. I simply told her that I work in the railway ministry. That's why I avoided addressing the public in her presence.

He continued, explaining his rationale, " My mother is unaware that I am a minister. She is simple, social, and homely lady. If she were aware of my actual position, she might start recommending people to me, and I would find it difficult to refuse her requests. I cannot refuse anything to my mother. In such circumstances, she might become inadvertently arrogant, which I do not want. I cannot deny my mother's requests, nor can I accept undue recommendations.

The heartfelt response left everyone stunned as it showcased the extraordinary moral character of Lal bahadur Shastri. In recognition of his outstanding qualities, he was posthumously awarded the Bharat Ratna, India's highest civilian award, in 1966.

9. POSITIVITY UNLEASHED

YOUR HIDDEN POWER

Jonathan Petti, a young man, found himself lost in a reverie of his earlier life. He dearly missed his mother, who had passed away when he was just a teenager. Her health had been declining, but she remained deeply concerned for her family's well-being. Then, one fateful day, she suffered a severe heart attack and departed for the realm beyond, leaving no opportunity for them to rush her to the hospital.

Jonathan, his elder brother, and his father had leaned heavily on her. She had devoted her entire life to ensuring their happiness, finding joy in their well-being and sorrow inn their trouble.

Following her passing, they felt like orphans for about ten days. However, his father soon rose to the occasion, taking on the roles of both a father and a mother. He began to care for their health, education, diet, and the upkeep of the household, much like their mother had. He became more than just a father, he became a mother figure as well.

From their early years, both Jonathan and his brother had been carefree, undisciplined, and mischievous under the loving guidance of their mother. Given their fathers' advanced age, he struggled to manage their newfound independence.

At this point, they became passive observers of unfolding events. They had countless complaints when their mother was alive --- complaints about the quality of dinner, the lack of playtime, the taste of their lunch boxes, and the state of their uniforms. Their mother always responded with a smile and fulfilled their wishes.

In the twilight years, their father dedicated his full attention to ensuring their happiness and guiding them towards responsible behavior. However, as the demands of playing both paternal and maternal roles became overwhelming for him, he decided to seek help and appointed a governess for this purpose.

The governess, a widow but sweet by nature, initially did not win their hearts. However, as time passed, she endeared herself to them with her love and affection. Like their mother, she was very particular about their diet and food. She would rise early in the morning, serve them breakfast in bed, prepare for their baths, iron their clothes, polish their shoes, and neatly pack their lunch boxes. Both brother couldn't believe whether the food was cooked by their mother or the governess. It was sumptuous, delicious, and mouth-watering.

As the time moved forward, Jonathan's elder brother went to USA for his postgraduate studies, leaving Jonathan alone in his school. The absence of his brother left him feeling isolated, and old memories haunted his mind. He lost interest in his studies, sports, and even stopped watching TV. Concerned about his health, his father decided to send him to a hostel.

Jonathan's elder brother was in USA, and Jonathan was admitted to a hostel. His father had done his best to secure admission to a prestigious college for a Law degree, bearing the heavy cost of his education and hostel fees. However, Jonathan always felt uncomfortable.

He faced numerous challenges and obstacles, including issues with hostel's food, difficulties in adjusting, personal helplessness, distress, changes in eating and sleeping habits, and many other issues. Every situation had its own unique challenges, and the same holds true for the life you live at home and the life you live in a hostel. Jonathan dug deep into the memories of his family life, recollecting, " I remember that during my school days, I always eagerly waited the sumptuous food prepared by my mother. " He longed to savor homemade food and bask in a loving environment under the protective embrace of his parents.

Every situation has its dual aspects, and this holds true whether you're living at home or in a hostel. We must embrace the side of the coin that fate flips for us. Jonathan delves deep into the recesses of his family memories. As I reminisce about those bygone days, I recall how, how during my school years, I eagerly waited the sumptuous meals my mother used to lovingly prepare. The prospect of homemade food filled me with longing, particularly when I was fed up with with the fare at the hostel. I decided to pay an unannounced visit home, my heart earnestly craving the comfort of home-cooked meals and the loving embrace of my parents.

My decision to return home from the hostel was a spontaneous one, and I didn't inform anyone about it. One of my mother's endearing habits was to swiftly whip up a meal as soon as I returned from school. On the day of my unexpected arrival from the hostel, it was my father who greeted me, his face beaming with joy. Uncertain about what to do, he immediately thought, of my mother and headed to the kitchen to prepare something for me. It was a touching display of a father's love for his son, one that the housekeeper, who was eager to prepare a delicious meal for me, observed keenly. However, due to my father's intense desire to care for me, she remained a silent spectator.

Once the food was set on the dinning table, my father invited me to sit down, and he joined me, closely watching as I relished the divine flavors crafted by his skilled hands. I finished my meal quietly and began washing the dishes, all the while aware of my father's attentive gaze.

Then, our housekeeper stepped forward, gently taking the plate from my hands and placing it in the dishwasher. She took my hand and guided me to the sofa, where we both took a seat.

" I understand that you didn't enjoy the food," she said softly." I apologize for letting your father cook for you; it's a testament to his enduring love for you."

I remained still and unmoving upon hearing her words. "What do you mean ?" I asked.

"Papa is a great cook, and the food he prepared was fantastic and delicious, " I explained sincerely. " I genuinely enjoyed it. I love his cooking."

"Don't lie. Your expression doesn't match your words, " she responded skeptically.

"No, it's true, " I insisted. " I savored every bite, and the unique flavors lingered in my mouth. The aroma of the spices he uses only made me hungrier. I've even praised his cooking to all my friends."

Really? She inquired, her tone slightly sarcastic. " You praise his cooking to your friends?"

I swear I do, I replied firmly.

She then shifted her focus. " And what about my cooking?"

You're an amazing cook too, and I enjoy your food even more, " I admitted.

She gazed at my face with surprise, and after a moment, she said, "You always eat so quickly, never saying anything. You never told your father or me that you liked our cooking, so I thought you rushed through your meals because you didn't enjoy them"

"It's true that I eat quickly, " I confessed, " but it's only because I can't resist the temptation of fishing such delicious food as fast as possible."

"Then you should have appreciated your father and me, " She said.

"Remember one thing, " she continued, " whenever someone does something kind for you, it's essential to express your gratitude and thank that person. If you don't express your thanks, they might assume you dislike their actions, and they may stop doing those kind deeds for anyone."

Her words deeply resonated with me, and her wisdom touched my heart. From that day forward, I made it a point to thank everyone for even the smallest gestures of kindness, whether their actions directly benefited me or not. This habit of expressing gratitude became a part of who I was, I couldn't pinpoint when it transformed into something magical.

The magic began to manifest in my life. People started to like me more, engage in conversations with me, share with me, and become friendlier. I found myself happier than ever before. My teachers, friends, relatives, and more individuals now expressed their love for me. Upon returning home after attending the farewell ceremony at my hostel before leaving for good, I discovered a bundle of cards filled with well-wishes. "Thanks, Dad and Governess," I said instinctively.

But my father and our housekeeper smiled and replied, "We didn't arrange these cards for you. They are from your classmates, teachers, and other hostel staff. They consider you the best student who understands the value of other and reciprocates with gratitude. These two simple words, ' THANK YOU"; have made tremendous difference, transforming those who were once put off by your ungratefulness into great appreciations."

That's the power of appreciation. When you possess it, everything in the world feels right, but in its absence, life seems empty. My father went on to explain that people who practice gratitude experience fewer physical discomfort, sleeps better, exhibit, happiness, energy, optimism, and empathy. When gratitude becomes a s central code value in your life, it empowers you to face any situation was grace, dignity, and hope.

It's easy to express gratitude for the good moments, but only those who can thank adversity will truly savor a satisfying life. Gratitude possesses the remarkable ability to transform negatives into positives.

10. ACCEPT CHALLENGES

Amit and Sumit, close friends sharing the same school, eagerly embraced the chance to become part of National Cadet Corps (NCC) , all thanks to their teacher's encouragement. The NCC, an abbreviation for the National Cadet Corps, was intricately linked to the Indian Military Cadet Corps. It frequently extended its its arms to students from diverse educational institutions, with the aim of nurturing their potential of future roles in safeguarding India's security. NCC training camps were periodically orchestrated to equip students with vital life skills. Propelled by their shared passion for serving their nation, Amit and Sumit eagerly enrolled in the NCC program.

Two months into their NCC journey, a pivotal camp was held in a wooded area, primarily designed to cultivate self-confidence in participants. Amit and Sumit eagerly anticipated this camp and actively participated. After initial classroom instructions, they were instructed to embark on a challenging trek through the forest.

On the designated day, their instructor summoned them to the starting point of the trek. True to their disciplined nature, Amit and Sumit arrived promptly. A signboard displayed the various routes leading from the starting point to the endpoint of the trek. The instructor pointed to the board and explained, " Your task is to begin here and reach the endpoint of the trek. The time it takes you to complete this challenge will also influence next week's test results."

Both of them willingly accepted the challenge, seeking the instructor's blessings before setting off. With well-wishes from their mentor , they began the race, sprinting at remarkable speed in their quest to finish the task as swiftly as possible. As they progressed, they reached crucial decision point where the path split into two options. The signboard indicated one path as longer yet easier, while the other was shorter but more demanding. Amit and Sumit had to choose between the path of convenience and the path of challenge.

Sumit chose to follow a clear and easily navigable path, while Amit opted for the shorter yet more challenging route. Amit's chosen path was riddled with obstacles such as fallen logs, wide trenches, and numerous other hurdles. Nevertheless, it offered a quicker way to reach the trek's endpoint. Sumit, opting for the simpler, unobstructed path, was the first to complete the trek within the specified time frame. He felt a sense of cleverness and satisfaction as he effortlessly passed through the course, skillfully avoiding all the hindrances and obstacles of the challenging path. Amit on the other hand, faced a prolonged journey to reach the endpoint. He had to navigate through a path fraught with difficulties, obstacles, ditches, and trenches, engaging in a constant battle with the arduous terrain. When Amit eventually reached the track's endpoint, Sumit proudly remarked, " I am glad I chose the easier path; the difficult one could have delayed my progress.' Sumit celebrated his triumph in the first round of the race by patting himself on the back and dancing with joy, While Amit stood in silence, observing his friend's contentment.

The following week, both Sumit and Amit were tasked with reaching a different location for the second leg of the race. This new location was situated within a forest, right at the edge of a deep and narrow gorge with steep, imposing sides. The instructor issued a stern warning, stating, "You must leap across to the other side of this gorge." The students were taken aback as they surveyed the intimidating expanse before them, spanning just a few meters in width. Sumit felt disoriented by the sheer width of the gorge and wrestled with the decision of whether to take this risky leap. Success would make him sole victor, but he couldn't help but contemplate the dire consequences of failure - a potentially serious injury if he tumbled into the valley below. His thoughts were fixated on the potential fallout from an unsuccessful jump, and this fear overpowered his resolve. Ultimately, he decided to step back, opting out of the challenge.

Turning his gaze towards Amit, the instructor observed that Amit was in a serious and contemplative mood. Amit vividly recalled the obstacles he had conquered in the first round of the race, including jumping over large logs and deep ditches. This memory filled him with hope. Amit meticulously studied the gorge, took a deep breath, and calculated his run-up. With determination, he sprinted towards the edge of the gorge and, in the blink of an eye, launched himself into the air. His leap seemed almost instantaneous, and with incredible skill, he successfully cleared the gap.

Other students who had also participated in this test, with a few managing to succeed while the majority fell short of contemplating it. The instructor took the opportunity to elucidate the purpose behind the test. The test had been designed in two distinct rounds. In the first round, students were given the choice to select either an easy or a difficult path. The difficult path had been meticulously crafted to serve as a preparation for the challenges that lay ahead in the second round. Those who opted for the easier route were able to complete it solely because of its simplicity, but the subsequently found themselves ill-prepared to conquer the more demanding second path.

Th instructor imparted a valuable lesson to the students; embracing challenges unlocks doors to significant breakthroughs and reveals hidden opportunities within them. Avoiding problems or evading the core issues merely prolongs the healing process. Life invariably presents us with challenges, ranging from minor obstacles to major hurdles. Many people tend to evade their problems, seeking quick and effortless solutions, only to become throughout our lives, we will never reach our full potential. However, by confronting the world head-on, with all its risks and challenges, we open ourselves up to limitless possibilities.

11. Value of Money

In a countryside village, there lived a dedicated and principled entrepreneur renowned for his unwavering integrity and tireless work ethic. The local residents held him in the highest esteem, appreciating his consistent readiness to lend a hand to those facing adversity. He labored relentlessly, overcoming countless obstacles, societal indifference, and numerous hurdles to establish his business, all while preserving his benevolent character.

This devoted businessman was also a father, nurturing a profound aspiration for his son to follow in his footsteps, laboring diligently and earning an honest livelihood. He yearned for his son to craft a reputation as unblemished as his own and attain a respected status in society. However, contrary to his aspirations, his son fell into the company of misguided individuals, evolving into wayward youth.

Not only did his son affiliate with detrimental crowd, but he also cultivated a repertoire of undesirable habits. Whenever his father requested his involvement in the family enterprise, he was armed with a litany of excuses to shrink his responsibilities. He held his father in high regard solely for his wealth, opting to fritter away his days gallivanting with unsavory companions. He lavished exorbitant sums of money to entertain his sycophantic friends, asserting dominance in the process. At the slightest hint of disrespect from any of his associates, he would unleash tantrums and adopt a domineering demeanor. His actions extended to physical confrontations, verbal abuse, and other behaviors that left those around him feeling embarrassed. Within the confines of his home, he remained a perpetual complainer from the moment he awoke. As he grew accustomed to reckless spending, he started squandering money at the insistence of his friends. This conduct, along with his son's actions, became a major source of concern for his father. Observing his hard-earned money dissipate due to his wayward son troubled him deeply. He clung to the hope that his son would mature and assume responsibilities for the family business, affording him and his wife the opportunity to embark on a long-awaited pilgrimage.

The man experienced a growing sense of disappointment and disconnection from his son due to the young man's lavish spending habits. One day, he decided to confront his son about his financial recklessness, hoping to teach him the value of honest earnings. He made a stern demand, telling his son that he must leave the house and earn a single rupee by evening; otherwise, he would not be allowed to stay in the family home or receive any food.

The son, unprepared for such a daunting challenge, pleaded his father to reconsider, but the father remained resolute in his decision. He was determined to instill a sense of financial responsibility in his child. Faced with his father's unwavering stance, the son felt helpless and broke into tears,

Unbeknownst to them, the mother had been silently witnessing the ordeal. Unable to bear her son's distress, she secretly gave him a one-rupee coin and instructed him to leave the house for the day, returning in the evening and presenting the coin as id he had earned it through his own efforts

The son was overjoyed to have the money from his mother. He left the house to spend the day with his friends and returned in the evening , offering the coin to his father. However, he was stopped at the gate and denied entry until he produced the required money. Panicking he produced the one-rupee coin for his father.

Their residence was an impressive, spacious place with a well in the open courtyard for water supply. The father instructed his son to toss the money into the well, a command the son promptly obeyed without hesitation. This routine repeated daily, with son receiving money from his other and obediently tossing it into the well as directed.

Over time, the father, aware of his wife's deep affection for their only son, grew suspicious and eventually uncovered the truth. He sent his wife to her father's house for a few days, leaving the son in a difficult predicament.

Feeling lost and uncertain, the son realized he had never contributed to his father's business and struggled to earn even a single rupee. His only option was to follow his father's orders and work diligently to earn money. Failure to do so meant being barred from entering the house and denied food, forcing him to understand the importance of hard work.

He searched for odd jobs but faced rejections due to his lack of experience. Eventually, he resorted to becoming a daily laborer. After two hours of strenuous work, carrying a heavy load like a porter, he managed to earn one rupee. Ecstatic, he kissed the coin and carefully kept it in his pocket. Upon returning home, he eagerly handed the money to his father, hoping for recognition for his hard work. However, the father, unmoved, instructed him to toss the coin into the well once again, just as before.

The son felt confusion and pain, as if sharp objects were pricking his body. He remembered the strenuous efforts he had put in to earn one rupee coin, and the idea of throwing it away seemed unjust.

In response to his father's request, the son expressed his anguish, saying, "I've toiled tirelessly today, every part of my body aches, and I've sweated profusely to earn this money. It goes against my very nature to cast it away. Regardless of the circumstances, I cannot bring myself to part with it." He firmly refused to comply with his father's directive and safeguarded the coin within their home, emphasizing, " I've kept the money safe. I simply cannot part with it."

With those words, the father was immensely pleased. His son had indeed understood the true value of money. It is often the challenges and struggles in life that mold us into the individuals we are meant to become. Without these obstacles, a smooth journey might weaken our inner strength, hindering us from reaching our full potential.

12. WORTH OF A MAN

In a distant village in India, there lived a highly skilled carpenter who was known by the name Kalu Ram but affectionately called Kalu by all. His woodworking craftmanship was nothing short of extraordinary, as he created intricately carved wooden pieces that earned admiration far and wide. His workshop was stocked with substantial inventory of high-quality wood.

Kalu's son Rahul, was a 10th-grade student blessed with a brilliant mind, but he was also known for his insatiable curiosity. His teachers often found themselves perplexed by his unrelenting stream of challenging questions, often delving into realms of knowledge beyond their own understanding. His voracious appetite for reading led him to explore the depths of truth-seeking literature.

One day as Rahul sat in his father's workshop, observing the transformation of rough wooden logs into magnificent creations, his attention was captivated by a particular wooden idol. Impressed, he turned to his father and asked about its price. Without waiting for a response, he continued to inquire about the cost of a nearby wooden frame and an adjacent flowerpot, with each question seamlessly leading into the next.

Taken aback by the rapid succession of questions from his son, Kalu struggled to provide answers. Just as he was about to contemplate the responses, Rahul posed yet another profound question, one that would challenge even the sharpest intellects.

Kalu, who had been busy attending to his customers, paused his work to gaze at his son's earnest face, astonished by his profundity of such a question from a young boy. Surprised by his intriguing query, he inquired, " Why ? What prompts you to ask such a question ?"

Young Rahul responded thoughtfully, " You see, dad, everything in this world is assigned some value. WE assess most things based on their worth. So, shouldn't a person also have a value ? That's why I'm asking what is the value of a man ?

Kalu pondered the question for a moment before replying, " Son, the worth of a human being is immeasurable. It is beyond calculation, and we can not assign a value to a person."

Rahul persisted, saying ,"But my teacher taught us that all human beings are equally valuable and important. If everything else has different values, why are all humans treated as equally valuable and important ?"

Kalu acknowledged, "Your teacher is correct."

However, Rahul found himself struggling to reconcile his teacher's words with his father's response. Dissatisfied, he continued, " if all humans are equal, why do we have rich and poor in this world?" Why are some less fortunate than Others? Why do some become servants while others are masters ?"

Upon hearing this question, Kalu remained silent for a moment, grappling with the challenge of finding a suitable answer. He realized that explaining profound philosophical concepts to a child was daunting task. Unable to provide a straightforward response, he devised a plan and instructed his son to retrieve a log of wood from the storeroom.

The young boy promptly ventured into the storeroom and retrieved a rough log of wood. The father observed the log attentively and posed a question to his son, " In your opinion, what should be the price of this piece of rough wood you've brought from the storeroom ?"

The son scrutinized the piece of wood closely and responded, " It's just a rough piece of wood suitable for burning, so it shouldn't be worth more than Rs. 200/-"

"Your assessment is spot on, My son, As a mere piece of rough wood, it should indeed be priced at no more than two hundred rupees. But what if we were to craft a walking stick from this wood, intended for use by elderly? What would they be worth then?

“Of course, their price would increase because of the efforts put into carving, so they might fetch around Rs. 1000/-‘

“And if I were to fashion a finely crafted pillar for use in a temple, what would its value be?”

The boy found himself perplexed, attempting to calculate the cost of a carved temple pillar as he counted on his fingers. After thoughtful consideration, he replied, “Well, it would cost significantly more. Carving a pillar would require a great deal of effort.”

“Very astute, my son. Now you understand that the worth of wood can change based on what can be crafted from it and its intended use.”

The father proceeded to convey a profound lesson to his son, stating , :Likewise a person’s worth isn’t solely determined by their current situation, but rather by thcir capacity to shape their own destiny. It hinges on the efforts they invest in crafting future. Should one settle for their present circumstances without pursuing growth, their vale wanes, rendering them without significance, as they avoid facing the challenges as hardships that lead to finely sculpted life.

We often nurture lofty aspirations and establish grand life objectives, only to become disheartened when we contemplate our current reality. We begin to perceive ourselves as significant and avoid of worth, allowing negativity to take root in our minds when confronted with life's trials. We tend to forget our immense potential and the fact that life teems with opportunities. Sometimes, these opportunities knock at our door, yet in our desolation, we neglect to open the doors of our wisdom.

Indeed many times in life, conditions may not be ideal, but adverse circumstances cannot diminish our inherent worth as human beings. The key lies in our unwavering commitment to self-improvement and acquisition of valuable skills, thereby enhancing our value, much like how a piece of wood gains worth by becoming more useful."

13. Embracing Empathy

Throughout the annals of history, we encounter instances where cruelty held sway. Monarchs and rulers once devised horrifying methods to punish those they deemed transgressors, often resorting to torture, brutality, and inhumanity. The pages of history are replete with tales of crucifixions, burnings, stoning, and even unspeakable practices like rat torture, where the suffering of others knew no bounds. In addition, their methods of punishment included boiling in water or oil and crushing by elephants.

In more recent times, we've borne witness to disturbing instances of exceptionally cruel and torturous punishments. A grim illustration can be found in the actions of the current North Korean leader, dictator Kim Jong-Un. He orchestrated the execution of his uncle, Jang Sung Taek, and his associates through a horrifying method known as " Quan Jue" or " execution by dogs. "The barbaric process involved stripping Kim Jong-Un and five of his aides bare before hurling them into a cage alongside 120 emaciated dogs that had endured three days of starvation. What followed was a gruesome, hour-long ordeal during which famished dogs ruthlessly tore apart and devoured Jang and his associates. This horrifying spectacle was personally overseen by Kim Jong-Un and witnessed by 300 senior officials.

This harrowing incident stands as a chilling example of the extreme brutality associated with the North Korean regime. At the time of their execution, Jang held the position of vice-chairman of North Korea. Their alleged transgressions were linked to political motivations and accusations of disloyalty to the ruling party, underscoring the depths of cruelty that can emerge in such circumstances.

In a world where cruelty often prevails, the presence of benevolent and compassionate individuals can appear scarce. Let me share a story that exemplifies the enduring value of kindness, even when extended to animals. Once upon a time, there ruled a king whose cruelty and injustice knew no bounds. He took pleasure in devising new, cruel methods of torment innocent people for his personal amusement. On one occasion, as he ventured out to inspect his kingdom, he encountered a man who chose not to rise and bow his head in deference to the king. According to the kingdom's law, every citizen was expected to stand and show respect as the king passed by.

This act of defiance resulted in severe punishment the man. Stripped of his clothing and tightly bound with ropes, he was suspended over a blazing fire until his body was charred to a gruesome resemblance, much like a roasted chicken. The cruel king, surrounded by his officials and family members, watched the callous delight, treating this horrific event as though it were a form of entertainment.

Sadly, it later emerged that the victim was blind, unable to perceive the world around him. In tragic twist of fate, the innocent soul had borne the brunt of a fault he never committed. This story serves as a poignant reminder of the ever-present necessity for kindness, compassion, and fairness, especially in a world where those in power bear the responsibility of safeguarding and caring for their subjects.

The cruelty of the monarch had grown so unbearable that his subjects fervently wished for either his demise or his removal from the throne. The, a fateful day arrived when he summoned all his subjects to the assembly hall, instilling an atmosphere of anxiety and dread among the citizens. They feared the worst, expecting impending doom. To their astonishment the once cruel king declared, " I have chosen a new path."

With a solemn vow of " No more cruelty," he pledged to his people. However, his proclamation was met with skepticism, as years of tyranny had eroded trust. Yet, the king remained true to his word. His demeanor underwent a remarkable transformation, displaying unprecedented kindness. He began to pardon a transgression that once warranted death sentences. The remarkable change in the king's behavior became the subject of the kingdom's conversation, igniting curiosity about the source of his newfound benevolence.

Cruelty had once brought the king delight, and he had reveled in devising innovative methods to torment even the innocent. As time passed, suspicion continued to linger among the populace. After several months of observing the king's transformation, one of his ministers finally mustered the courage to inquire about the reason behind his change of heart.

Until then , no one had dared to question the king. The Minister's audacity in challenging his decision was remarkable. The king fixed his penetrating gaze upon the minister, who trembling with fear and expecting his imminent demise, swiftly prostrated himself and implored for forgiveness. To everyone's surprise, the king smiled and reassured him, saying, "Fear nit, you are safe. You have committed no wrong. I understand that your question mirrors the curiosity shared by all present here about the catalyst for my changed behavior. I shall reveal the secret behind my transformation, " Please take your seat."

With that, the king proceeded to narrate a story involving one of his close friends, who happened to be the ruler of a neighboring small state. The friend had a penchant for hunting dogs and gruesome tradition of staging elaborate public executions as form of punishment. This practice served dual purpose for him; it resulted in the execution of the condemned individual and provided him with a sadistic thrill from witnessing the brutal demise of an unfortunate soul. The king confessed to adopting this method, inspired by a particular incident related to him by his friend, as the key to his own transformation.

The king narrated that my royal friend, who also holds the title of king, maintains a squadron of well-trained dogs. Under a strict rule, anyone who commits an error in their actions faces the prospect of being thrown to these voracious canines. To ensure their readiness to consume any individual at any given moment, these dogs are intentionally deprived of food for three days.

This rule was once applied to one of the king's own advisors, and on another occasion, a wise minster presented an opinion that ultimately proved to be incorrect. In response. The king ordered his soldiers to cast the minister into the midst of the famished dogs, sealing his fate with a final decree.

Desperate for mercy, the wise minister implored the king, " Please, I have faithfully served to for two decades. Spare me just this once, I solemnly vow never to repeat such a mistake."

The king remained steadfast, reluctant to forgo the gruesome spectacle of an execution. The minister pleaded once more, beseeching the king to delay his execution by a mere ten days. \

He implored, " I humbly request a ten-day stay of execution, Your majesty."

After considering the minister's long and and impeccable service spanning two decades, the king agreed to the postponement. The wise minister then approached the dog trainer and made an unusual request.

He asked, " Please grant me permission to spend ten days with the dogs; I wish to serve them during this time," Having received assistance from the minister on multiple occasions in the past, the dog trainer found the request perplexing but decided to take the risk, given their prior interactions.

He inquired , " What purpose this serve ? Your fate is sealed, and your days are numbered."

The minister replied , " I will explain later.'

The trainer ultimately agreed, saying, " Very well, the choice is yours."

Over those ten days, the minister dedicated himself to the dog's care, tending their needs, feeding them, bathing them, and providing every possible comfort. He engaged in playful interactions, tickled his furry companions, and meticulously attended to their well-being. He even shared their sleeping quarters, immersing himself fully in their world, forging a deep bond with each and every dog.

After the ten-day period had passed, the king, accompanied by his guards, approached the minister with a sense of anticipation. The king remarked, "Now, it's time for the spectacle. I am eager to witness how your body will be torn apart, piece by piece, by my ravenous dogs."

Following the king's command, the minister was cast into the enclosure containing the famished dogs. The king along with his family members, ministers, high ranking officials, and several prominent individuals from the kingdom, had gathered to witness this event, reminiscent of past gruesome execution. Every one was eager to observe the horrific spectacle of these hungry dogs devouring a living human being. As they watched with rapt attention, a profound shock awaited the king, his family, and his soldiers.

The famished dogs stood in an eerie silence, their moments strangely halted. A few even sat peacefully amidst the mist, showing no sign of aggression. The dog trainer, perplexed by this uncommon behavior, found himself in a state of bewilderment. These ravenous dogs had never hesitated to pounce on their prey before. Intrigued by their unusual activity, he tried to incite them, urging them to attack the minister. To his astonishment, the hungry dogs responded by barking at him. The king, too, was mystified by the sight of his normally voracious dogs refusing their customary feast of fresh human flesh and blood.

Fueld by anger, the king demanded of minister, " What have you done to my loyal hounds ? These hunting dogs have never shown mercy to their prey before."

Remaining composed and undisturbed by the menacing presence of the hunting dogs, the minister replied, " I have served these dogs for a mere ten days, and they have not forgotten my service. In contrast, I have served you faithfully for two decades, and it seems you have forgotten all that I have done for you."

The gathered assembly took note of the minister's words, and the unexpected behavior of the dogs began to weigh heavily on the king's conscience.

The king then declared, " I have learned a profound life lesson from these animals, which were one employed by my friend to instill fear, terror, and cruelty among his own subjects. This, and only this, is the secret behind my transformation."

With this revelation, the minister was released, and all the cruel and senseless rules were promptly revoked. The lesson learned was clear: Always exhibit kindness towards both people and animals and never forget the goodness extended to us by others.

14. Life is an Echo: What you give comes back to you.

During my school days, a teacher once imparted a valuable lesson, citing a saying whose origin I can't quite recall, but its wisdom lingers vividly in my memory. The adage goes as follows:

" What we send out comes back to us. What we sow, we reap. What we give, we get. What we see in others already exists in us. Remember, life is an echo. It always gets back to us. So always give goodness."

These words are akin to the biblical truth, " You reap what you sow." Just as one plant seeds and later reaps the harvest that corresponds to the type of seeds sown - corn doesn't yield olives - our actions, whether good or bad, bear consequences.

Winston Churchill eloquently summarized this concept, stating,

" We make a living by what we get, but we make a life by what we give."

In essence, our deeds, our kindness, and our generosity reflects back on us in various ways, ultimately shaping the quality of our lives.

This idea can be best exemplified through a heartwarming story:-

Once, a priest discovered an unconscious person on the temple stairs. Driven by his devotion to helping those in need, he nursed that stranger back to health with selfless care, fully embodying his role as a man of God. The priest acted out of pure human duty, without any expectation of personal gain. He lived by the belief that, as the head priest had once told him, " Someone will live a happier life merely because we take the time to share what we have to give."

Time flowed on, and one day, the priest's door was vigorously knocked upon. When he opened the door, he was astonished to find the the very man whose life he had saved. The man, a farmer, had brought a bucket filled with the finest fruits from his garden as a gift. He respectfully offered the fruits to the priest, expressing his deep gratitude and acknowledging the priest's selfless act.

The priest, humbled and touched by the gesture, felt that he didn't deserve to keep the gift. Instead, he believed it should be offered to the head priest who had imparted valuable life lessons to him. But the farmer insisted that the gift was meant for the priest who had saved his life. With a warm smile, the priest accepted the fruits.

Although he had not enjoyed such high-quality fruits for a long time, the priest decided to offer the gift to the head priest. This act was not only an expression of gratitude but also a way to share the joy he felt.

The head priest, in turn, was delighted with the gift of fresh fruits. He thought of his family, realizing that he hadn't been able to provide them with such treats for a while. He decided to share the gift with his loved ones, aiming to bring happiness into their lives. However, his thoughts soon turned to the Head of the village, who had been ill and was unable to obtain fresh fruits. The head priest saw this as an opportunity to bring some joy to the ailing man's life.

So, the priest presented the fruits to the Head of the village as a gift, hoping they would bring some comfort. But the story doesn't end there; the sick man being cared for by a kind villager, chose to pass on the gift to the person who had selflessly served him, offering care, medical help, and nourishing food. In this way, the cycle of giving and kindness continued, as the fruits found their way from one grateful heart to another, reflecting the profound truth that " what we send out comes back to us" and that" life is an echo" of our deeds.

In school time my teacher told me about a famous saying by a wise man, though I do not remember the name of the wise man but still remember his words full of wisdom and repeated it here below:

"What we send out comes back to us. What we sow, we reap. What we give, we get. What we see in others already exists in us. Remember, life is an echo. It always gets back to us. So always give goodness".

The above saying is a Biblical truth

"You reap what you sow" You plant the seeds (sow), and then later you gather the resulting harvest (reap). The harvest that you reap depends on the kind of seeds you sow If you sow corn, you will not reap olives"

In the words of Winston Churchill "We make a living by what we get, but we make a life by what we give."

In short, the meaning of all the above quotes is whatever deeds we perform, whether good or bad, we have to certainly bear the fruit of the same. It can very easily be explained by the following story:-

Story: Life an echo

Once, a priest found a person unconscious on the stairs of a temple. He escorted him to his home and looked after his health providing all sorts of comforts only to save his life. His efforts to help an unknown person were driven by the force of his being a man of God to deliver goods to all in need of help. He thought it to be a human duty without any self-interest. He did it and forgot it remembering golden words of the head priest "Someone will live a happier life merely because we took the time to share what we had to give."

Time passed away and one day the door of the priest was knocked hard. When the priest opened up he saw the same person whose life was saved by him. A farmer by profession the man had brought a bucket full of fresh fruits of his garden and politely offered fruits to the pries and said:

"Sir, these fruits are the finest my garden has produced. I have come to offer them as a gift. The priest accepted the gift and said, I do not deserve to keep this gift with me. I must offer it to the head priest who taught me the best lessons in life. He will be delighted with this gift. I must offer these fruits to the head priest.

Sorry sir, but I have brought this gift only for you. You are the person who saved my life when there was no help available nearby. I know you were not having much money to provide me medical help but you spent all that you possessed just to save the life of an unknown person. I wish you must keep it with you.

The priest smiled and went inside his house holding the gift in his hands. Though he had never seen such good quality fruits and had also not eaten good fruits for long, yet he decided to deliver the gift to the head priest, who always encouraged him with words of wisdom.

The head priest was very pleased with a bucket of fresh fruits. He wanted to please his family members with this gift because he was not able to buy good fruits for them. He wished to make them all happy with this unique gift. Instantly he remembered that the Head of the village was sick and was suffering from illness for quite some time. Living in a remote area it was not easy for him to get fresh fruits. His condition was deteriorating day by day. The head priest decided to give fruits to the Head of the village. Who knows, they may bring some joy to his life.

The priest presented these fruits to the Head of the village as a gift. But the fruits didn't stay with the sick man for long. One of the villagers was living with him with a purpose to help the head in his ill condition. He was the one who took good care of him, helped him in day to day activities. Provided him timely medicines as told by the village doctor and cooked food for him. The head of the village decided to pass on this gift to the villager who served him for long. Sure, the villager will be pleased to find such a good gift.

The villager was amazed to get such a fine gift. He had never seen fruits of such good quality. He was sure that these fruits cannot be appreciated more than the monk who had established the temple and spent his entire life in the welfare of common poor people. He would certainly appreciate this marvel of nature. It would be best if I offer this gift to the monk.

Several trainee monks were working hard to learn the lessons of doing good to the people on the earth. The monk selected the junior-most trainees and gave him the gift of fruits just to make him understand the work of nature in the smallest details of its creation.

The junior-most trainee remembered his old bad days. He had no house, nothing to eat or wear. He was wandering from place to place in search of some help. It was the temple where he got the shelter, food, and everything. He remembered the first time he came to the temple, and of the priest who had opened the gates for him. It was the gesture that allowed him to be among this community of people who knew how to value wonders of life.

He instantly took the fruits to the priest in the temple. Eat and enjoy the fruits. You spend your most time alone here in the temple, and these fruits will make you very happy.

It was a circle of good deeds that was completed. What the priest had given to others had come back to him. Thus the circle was closed; the circle of happiness and joy; which always shines brightly around generous people.

Someone has rightly said:

" The best portion of good man's life is his little, nameless, unremembered acts of kindness and love."

As per Bible "Do all the good you can, by all the means you can, in all the ways you can, in all the places you can, at all the times you can, to all the people you can, as long as ever you can"

The villager was filled with astonishment upon receiving such exquisite fruits. These were fruits of unparalleled quality; unlike any he had ever laid eyes on before. In his heart, he was convinced that these exceptional fruits were a tribute to the monk who had devoted his entire life to the welfare of the fortunate in their community. It was only fitting to present this remarkable gift to the monk.

Meanwhile, a group of young trainee monks was earnestly immersed in their lessons on the art of benevolence towards the people of the world. The elder monk, keen to impart the subtlest lessons of nature's work, singled out the most junior of the trainees and bestowed upon him this gift of fruits.

The junior trainee's thoughts turned to the difficult days of his past when he had been destitute, homeless, and in dire need of sustenance. It was the temple that had offered him refuge, nourishment, and clothing. His mind wandered back to the moment when the temple's priest had welcomed him, granting him entry into a community that understood how to cherish life's wonder. Without hesitation, he brought the fruits to the priest.

“Please, enjoy these fruits, “he said. “You spend much of your time alone in the temple, and these fruits are sure to bring you happiness.”

And so, a circle of goodwill was completed. What the priest had given to others had come back to him. This was the closure of avirtuous cycle, a circle of happiness and joy that perpetually radiates around those who exhibit generosity. It brought to mind a wise saying :

“ The best portion of good man’s life is his little, nameless, unremembered acts of kindness and love.”

In the words of the Bible:

“ Do all the good you can, by all the means you can, in all the ways you can, in all the places you can, at all the times you can, to all the people you can, as long as ever you can.”

15. Building a Bridge

This tale revolves around two brothers who had been neighbors and farming partners for countless years, their companionship unshaken until a single foolish disagreement tore them apart. Remarkably, it marked the very first significant dispute in their half-century of togetherness. Before that fateful day, they had always harmonious tended to their lands, freely exchanged wisdom and crops, and provided unwavering support in times of hardship. The dispute had its origins in a trivial misunderstanding, an unfortunate occurrence that can happen to anyone, However, regrettably, it escalated into a heated exchange of bitter words, leaving them in silence of weeks on end.

One morning, an unexpected visitor knocked at the elder brother's door. Upon opening it, he found an aged bearded carpenter, clutching a toolbox, standing before him. "I am in need of work, Sir, " the stranger remarked. "Do you require any repairs on your farm ? The elder brother replied with determination, "Yes, indeed. Onn the other side of the creek lies my younger brother's farm. Until recently, our properties were adjacent, enveloped in lush greenery. But de deliberately altered the course of the creek, creating a divide between us. I suspect it was an act of spite. However, I intend to retaliate ...."His voice resonated with determination as he continued, "Do you see those trees by the barn ? I want you to transform them into a formidable 10-foot-high fence. I want to ensure I never have to lay eyes on his face again."

The elderly carpenter pondered silently for several moments before finally saying, "I understand." The farmer then assisted the carpenter in transporting his tools and the timber, after which he departed for the city to attend to some errands. Upon his return later in the evening , he was met with and astonishing sight. As he reached the creek, the elder brother was left in a state of profound shock. His eye widened, rendering him utterly speechless.

Where a fence should have been standing, there now stood a bridge – an extraordinary and unique bridge, a true masterpiece adorned with meticulously carved railings. By chance, the young brother arrived at the same spot at that very moment. He hurried across the bridge and embraced his elder brother, exclaiming, " You're truly exceptional, constructing a bridge despite all I've said and done. "As the two brothers shared a heartfelt embrace, the aged carpenter gathered his tools and began to take his leave. Turning to the carpenter, the brothers implored, " Please stay with us a while longer. There are more tasks in need of your skilled touch. " I would have cherished the opportunity, kind sirs, replied the carpenter, " but have countless more bridges to craft and countless more things to mend in distant places.

This story reminds us that anger can sometimes distance us from our loved ones, and pride can overshadow our love. Let us be vigilant against these pitfalls. Embrace forgiveness and cherish what you have. Remember that the past is unchangeable, but the future holds the potential for transformation. No quarrel should tarnish a genuine connection. When necessary, build bridges and always cross them with a smile.

16. CREATING MIRACLES

In India, a long-standing tradition prevails in which every village hosts a communal gathering place known as a "Choupal." This Choupal serves as the heart of the community, bringing people together to address concerns, celebrate joyous events, mediate disputes under the guidance of village elders, and support one another in times of need.

The Gram Panchayat, the governing body responsible for the village's development, plays a pivotal role in addressing civic matters. However, the effectiveness of the Gram Panchayat largely hinges on the existence of the Choupal, which serves as a central meeting point for villagers on various occasions.

In the village of Sondhi in Bihar, Sarpanch Harpal leads the community with a strong emphasis on maintaining the Choupal premises. Over time, he observed that Mrs. Radha, who oversees the Choupal, appeared distracted and neglectful of her duties. Concerns arose within the village, with some suggesting her removal from her position. However, the majority opted for a different approach: they decided to investigate the reasons behind her inactivity.

After much discussion, the villagers arrived at a unanimous decision to assign a well-educated young man to investigate the matter. Yet, when this task was offered to several young men in the village, they declined, fearing it might be seen as disrespectful to Radha and her family. This dilemma persisted for several days as the village searched for a suitable investigator.

Ultimately, a young man approached the village Pradhan (head) and offered his services for the task. However, he harbored suspicions that his involvement might be misunderstood by the villagers. To ensure the investigation's legality, he set one condition: his role must remain confidential, with his name never to be disclosed. This agreement was solidified during a private conversation between him and the Pradhan.

Afterward, the young man commenced an extensive period of discreet observation of Radha's activities. He meticulously recorded the times she entered and left the Choupal. On one particular day, he made the decision to quietly shadow her as she left the Choupal and was astonished to find that she did not head straight home but instead made her way to a moneylender's shop. It became apparent that she was seeking a loan to purchase medicine for her seriously ill husband. He discreetly followed her until she reached her residence.

The scene that greeted him was nothing short of heart-wrenching. Radha's home was in a dire state, with children who appeared malnourished and were wearing tattered clothing. Her husband was in excruciating pain, and only after administering some medicine did he experience slight relief. The young man found it difficult to believe that, despite such challenging circumstances, Radha was still managing to fulfill her duties at the Choupal.

In this village, a long-standing tradition involved hosting an annual confederation where villagers collectively contributed to a lottery. Each villager would pitch in Rs. 200/- to form a fund. In a village of 500 residents, everyone eagerly participated in this lottery system. The accumulated sum would eventually be awarded to the fortunate winner.

On the day of the lottery draw, the atmosphere in the Choupal was filled with electric excitement. Each person wrote their name on a slip of paper and placed it into the lottery box. Amid this anticipation, the young man assigned to investigate hesitated as he wrote. His hesitation stemmed from the knowledge that Radha, the Choupal's cleaning lady, had a husband who was frail and ailing, in need of an upcoming surgery that they couldn't afford, causing Radha immense distress.

Although fully aware that the odds of winning were a mere three percent, the young man inscribed Radha's name on his paper, offering a silent prayer in his heart for her victory. The tension in the air was palpable as the Village Pradhan delved into the lottery box, eventually pulling out a slip. The young man held his breath, fervently hoping that Radha would be the recipient of the prize. With careful consideration, the Village Pradhan proceeded to announce the name of the fortunate winner.

To the collective delight of the villagers, Radha emerged as the fortunate winner, and the Choupal resounded with cheers of jubilation. She swiftly ascended the stage to accept her prize, her eyes glistening with tears. Overwhelmed by emotions, expressing her gratitude proved to be a formidable challenge. Every word that escaped her lips quivered, and she struggled to contain her surging feelings. Finally, she managed to convey, "I never imagined I could be so fortunate. This money means the world to me—a glimmer of hope for my husband."

Following the lottery game, in line with tradition, everyone present joined together for a joyous and lively celebration. Meanwhile, the young man who had inscribed Radha's name on the slip of paper approached the lottery box. He retrieved a slip and opened it casually, revealing Radha's name once more. His astonishment grew as he extracted several more slips from the lottery box. Despite the varying handwriting, he discovered that Radha's name adorned each one. His heart leaped with realization, understanding that a remarkable miracle had unfolded. However, he recognized that such miracles do not descend from the heavens; they are crafted by the hands and intentions of people.

17. BECOMING LARGER THAN LIFE

Once upon a time, there lived a humble man with his wife and six children. Their household was beset by financial difficulties, making it a daily struggle to make ends meet. In the vicinity, an affluent family enjoyed the luxuries of life, showering their children with every conceivable desire.

One fateful day, the children from both families noticed a group of individuals diligently erecting a grand tent in the town. Filled with curiosity, the children approached the workers and asked, "What is the purpose behind this colossal tent? Does it signify something extraordinary?"

The leader among the workers kindly informed them that the tent was being set up for a temporary puppet show. Townsfolk would have the opportunity to witness this marvelous spectacle by purchasing tickets. This news ignited immense excitement among all the children, as they eagerly anticipated a form of entertainment they had never experienced before. Without delay, the children of the destitute man hurried back home to share this significant event with their parents, filling their humble abode with joy.

Meanwhile, the affluent family's children arrived, brandishing currency notes, ready to purchase tickets for the show. They, too, anxiously awaited their father's return in the evening. As the day wore on, all the children impatiently waited to see if their father would arrive. Upon his return, the weary poor man sought respite on his bed, a daily routine where he was usually left undisturbed. However, the children's excitement got the better of them, and they implored their father for money to attend the puppet show. This intrusion upon his resting time was unprecedented, and the poor man felt a tinge of irritation. Nevertheless, he inquired about the reason for their fervent pleas. His wife explained the enticing entertainment show that had commenced in their town.

Upon hearing the desires of his family, the poor man reminisced about a time in his own childhood when he had enjoyed such a captivating show. Recalling the modest ticket prices from back then, he consented to take his entire family to the puppet show. Upon reaching the venue for the show, they encountered a substantial queue at the ticket counter. With no alternative, they too joined the line to purchase tickets for the event.

As time passed, only one more family remained in front of them at the ticket counter—a husband, a wife, and their single child. The husband frantically searched his pockets but couldn't find enough money to purchase tickets for his family. Disheartened by their predicament, this family graciously made way for the other family, who, like them, appeared less financially fortunate. This second family consisted of the poor man, his wife, and their six children, all probably under the age of 12. Despite their humble clothing, their attire was neat and well-maintained.

The children displayed remarkable manners, patiently queuing behind their parents, their excitement evident as they chatted animatedly about their first experience at a puppet show. It promised to be a significant highlight in their lives. At the front of the line stood the father and mother, radiating pride. The mother clung to her husband's hand, a look of admiration in her eyes, as if to convey, "You are my knight in shining armor." He reciprocated with a beaming smile, savoring the sight of his family's happiness.

When the ticket lady inquired about the number of tickets needed, the man proudly responded, "I would like to purchase six children's tickets and two adult tickets." The ticket lady then disclosed the total cost of all the tickets. At that moment, the man's wife released her grip on his hand, hanging low, and his lip began to tremble. Leaning closer, he inquired, "Could you please repeat that." The ticket lady reiterated the price, revealing that the man didn't have enough money to cover the cost of the tickets for his entire family.

Recognizing the predicament, a kind-hearted stranger among them reached into his pocket, retrieved a $20 bill, and discreetly dropped it on the ground. Bending down, he picked up the $20 bill and tapped the man on the shoulder, saying, "Excuse me, sir, this must have fallen out of your pocket," as he handed it to him.

The man understood the unspoken gesture of assistance. He wasn't asking for charity, but he deeply appreciated the support in this desperate, heart-wrenching, and embarrassing moment. Meeting the eye of the generous stranger, he held the $20 bill tightly in both hands. With trembling lips and tears streaming down his cheeks, he expressed his gratitude, "Thank you, thank you, sir. This means the world to me and my family."

The kind-hearted man, along with his family, returned to their car and headed home. The $20 that the compassionate stranger had given away was meant for their own tickets. Although they missed the puppet show that night, they carried a joy within them that far surpassed any entertainment the show could offer. On that day, their children learned the invaluable lesson of giving. They understood that the act of giving makes the giver greater than the receiver. To become larger than life, one must learn the art of giving.

The giver is indeed greater than the receiver. If we want to be large, larger than life, we must learn to give.

18 Seeds of Kindness

Cultivating Hope

In a quaint, serene village nestled among rolling hills and lush greenery, the tale of an elderly woman named Margaret unfolds. She had seen over eight decades of life, her hair shimmering like a moonbeam, her face etched with the lines of wisdom and age. Margaret had weathered the ebb and flow of seasons, her life marked by challenges.

Residing alone in a modest cottage at the village's edge, Margaret had no remaining family. Her meager income stemmed from a small vegetable garden she meticulously tended. Unfortunately, the produce from her garden was far from perfect – often misshapen, withered, or small in size, dissuading many villagers from purchasing her vegetables.

One sunny morning, as Margaret set up her humble vegetable stall in the village square, a compassionate soul named Thomas approached her. He had observed Margaret's struggles and decided to purchase some vegetables, despite their less-than-ideal appearance. Margaret was taken aback by his generosity and profusely thanked him.

Upon returning home with the vegetables, Thomas's wife, Sarah, couldn't conceal her annoyance. "Why did you buy these subpar vegetables, Thomas?" she exclaimed. "We can find better ones at the market. We're wasting our money."

Thomas sighed and gently sat Sarah down. He shared with her the depth of Margaret's predicament – an elderly woman living in dire circumstances, alone and unsupported. He said, "Our purchase might not be about the quality of vegetables, but it's about helping a poor old lady in need."

Sarah's heart softened as she absorbed Thomas's words. She realized the significance of their gesture and agreed to support Margaret by purchasing from her regularly.

News of Thomas's act of kindness spread throughout the village, prompting more villagers to follow his lead. They began buying vegetables from Margaret, not because they were of the highest quality, but out of a desire to lend a hand to a fellow villager in distress.

Margaret was overwhelmed with gratitude. A glimmer of hope kindled in her heart, knowing that her fellow villagers cared about her well-being. Increased sales allowed her to enjoy better meals and live more comfortably.

As days turned into weeks, Margaret felt compelled to give back to the community that had shown her such compassion. She invested in high-quality seeds and sought advice from experienced farmers in the village to enhance her gardening skills. With determination and hard work, Margaret's garden began to flourish, yielding some of the finest vegetables the village had ever seen.

To express her gratitude, Margaret offered her newly acquired, high-quality vegetables at discounted rates to her loyal customers. She aimed to ensure that everyone in the village had access to fresh, nutritious produce, regardless of their financial situation.

The villagers were thrilled with Margaret's generosity and the improved quality of her vegetables. They continued to support her, not out of pity but out of genuine admiration for her resilience and her commitment to giving back to the community.

Margaret's story became an inspiring example of how a small act of kindness from one person could set in motion a chain reaction of goodwill and positive change within an entire community. The once-forgotten elderly lady not only survived but also became a symbol of hope and unity in the village. She reminded everyone that sometimes, all it takes is a helping hand to transform a life and a community for the better.

19. KNOCK AT MY DOOR

Making a life line

In the charming neighbourhood of Rohin, where well-kept gardens and white picket fences adorned the houses, there was a distinct residence that caught my attention. It wasn't remarkable for its architectural splendour or extravagant landscaping; rather, it was a simple mailbox at the end of the driveway that set it apart. Painted in a cheerful shade of blue, this mailbox held a peculiar feature—it was intentionally blocked.

As the local newspaper delivery person, it was during one of my early morning rounds that I first spotted this unique mailbox. Intrigued, I couldn't resist the urge to investigate. I confidently knocked on the door, curious about who would respond.

Moments later, the door creaked open, revealing Mr. Banerji, an elderly man with wisps of gray hair and unsteady steps. He peered at me through his glasses, offering a warm but somewhat mischievous smile.

I inquired, "Sir, why is the mailbox entrance blocked?"

Leaning on his walking cane, Mr. Banerji replied, "I intentionally blocked it."

Perplexed, I asked, "May I ask why, Sir?"

With a smile, he explained, "I want you to deliver the newspaper to me every day—please knock on the door or ring the bell and hand it to me in person."

I was puzzled and remarked, "Sure, but that seems inconvenient for both of us and a waste of time."

He responded, "It's alright—I'll give you an extra Rs. 500 each month as a knocking fee. And if there ever comes a day when you can't knock on the door, please call the police."

Shocked, I questioned, "Why call the police?"

Mr. Banerji replied, "My wife passed away, my son is abroad, and I live here all alone. Who knows when my time will come?" At that moment, I noticed the old man's misty, moist eyes.

He continued, "I never read the newspaper. I subscribe to it to hear the sound of knocking or the doorbell ringing. To see a familiar face and exchange a few words and pleasantries."

With a firm grip on my hands, he made a heartfelt request, "Young man, please do me a favor. Here's my son's overseas number. If one day you knock on the door and I don't answer, please call my son to inform him."

Leaving Mr. Banerji's doorstep that morning, my heart was heavy with mixed emotions—compassion for his solitude and gratitude for the opportunity to bring a ray of human connection into my life.

As the days passed, I faithfully knocked on Mr. Banerji's door every morning, exchanging pleasantries and engaging in brief conversation. In the process, I learned about his life -- his days as a school teacher, his love for classic music, and the stories of his son's adventures abroad

One particularly chilly morning, Mr. Banerji handed me a cup of steaming tea. We sipped the tea together, our breaths visible in the crips air. He shared tales of his youth, and I talked about my dreams for the future. In those moments, the age gap between us seemed to disappear, and we were just two friends, sharing a quit moment.

Over time, I became more than just a newspaper delivery person to Mr. Banerji, I became a source of companionship and a lifeline to the outside world. Our interactions became a daily ritual that brightened both our lives.

One day, as I was about to leave, Mr Banerji turned somber, " Young , "he said , " I've been thinking about our conversations , and I've realized something important."

"What is it, Sir? I asked.

He smiled gently. " I have come to understand that life is not just about the big events or achievements, it's about the small moment of connection and kindness. And you, my friends, have given me the greatest gift --- a friend to share those moments with."

Moved by his words, I replied, You've given me a gift too, Mr. Banerji – the gift of perspective and the reminder that a simple act of knocking on a door can make a world of difference."

As time went on, our bond deepened, and Mr. Banerji's health began to deteriorate. I watched as he grew frailer with each passing day. But I was there with him, to knock on his door and check on him, just as he had asked.

One chilly winter morning , the door remained closed despite my persistent knocks. Panic gripped me as I called out of him. There was no response. Remembering Mr. Banerji's request, I reached for the overseas phone number he had given me.

His son answered, and I explained the situation. Within hours, his son arrived from abroad, and together, we entered the house. Mr. Banerji had peacefully passed away in his sleep, surrounded by the memories of our conversations and companionship.

As I stood there, looking at the empty chair where my dear friend used to sit, I realized the profound impact of our daily interactions. It wasn't just about delivering a newspaper, it was about delivering a sense of connection, warmth, and companionship to an elderly soul whon had been yearning for it.

After Mr. Banerji's passing, I continued my newspaper route, but it was never quite the same. I thought about the lessons he had ought me -- the importance of human connection, the significance of small acts of kindness, and the power of a simple knock on the door.

And so, it is a testament to the fact that in the hustle bustle of our modern lives, we forget about the simplest gestures that can make the most significant impact, whether it's a knock on the door, a friendly conversation, or a telephone or a WhatsApp video call. This may prove to be a significant act of kindness that can bring some smile on the faces of those living alone in solitude

As the days rolled by, I faithfully continued my daily ritual of knocking on Mr. Banerji's door each morning, engaging in warm pleasantries and delving into snippets of his life. During these moments, I learned about his former life as a schoolteacher, his deep affection for classical music, and the captivating tales of his son's adventures abroad.

On one particularly brisk morning, Mr. Banerji surprised me with a steaming cup of tea. We sipped the tea together, our breath visible in the crisp air, sharing stories of his youth and my dreams for the future. In those moments, the age gap between us seemed to dissolve, and we were merely two friends, relishing a quiet interlude.

Over time, I evolved from being a mere newspaper delivery person to Mr. Banerji. I became a source of companionship and a lifeline to the world outside. Our interactions became a cherished daily ritual that illuminated both our lives.

One day, as I was preparing to depart, Mr. Banerji's demeanour turned reflective. "Young one," he said, "I've been pondering our conversations, and I've come to realize something significant."

Curious, I asked, "What is it, Sir?"

He smiled gently and replied, "I've come to understand that life is not solely about grand events or achievements; it's about those small moments of connection and kindness. And you, my friend, have given me the greatest gift—a companion to share those moments with."

Touched by his words, I responded, "You've given me a gift too, Mr. Banerji—the gift of perspective and a reminder that a simple act of knocking on a door can make a world of difference."

As time passed, our bond deepened, but Mr. Banerji's health gradually declined. I watched as he grew frailer with each passing day, yet I remained there, faithfully knocking on his door as he had requested.

One chilly winter morning, the door stayed closed despite my persistent knocks. Panic washed over me as I called out for him, receiving no response. Recalling Mr. Banerji's instructions, I reached for the overseas phone number he had entrusted to me.

His son answered, and I explained the situation. Within hours, his son arrived from abroad, and together, we entered the house. Mr. Banerji had peacefully passed away in his sleep, surrounded by the memories of our conversations and companionship.

As I stood there, gazing at the empty chair where my dear friend used to sit, I grasped the profound impact of our daily interactions. It wasn't merely about delivering a newspaper; it was about delivering a sense of connection, warmth, and companionship to an elderly soul who had yearned for it.

After Mr. Banerji's passing, I continued my newspaper route, but it was never quite the same. I pondered the lessons he had imparted—the value of human connection, the significance of small acts of kindness, and the potency of a simple knock on the door.

It serves as a testament to the fact that in the whirlwind of our modern lives, we often overlook the simplest gestures that can have the most profound impact, whether it's a knock on the door, a friendly conversation, or a phone call or video chat. Such acts of kindness can bring smiles to the faces of those living in solitude.

20. BE A BIG JAR NOT A GLASS

IN a quaint village, there resided two inseparable friends, Ram and Sham. They were not just companions but shared a deep bond of camaraderie that defined their lives. Friendship, they believed, had a unique way of overlooking the boundaries of logic and sensibility. Sometimes, their friendship manifested in playful pranks they would pull on each other.

One evening, as they sat down for dinner together, Sham decided to play a little trick on Ram. Unbeknownst to Ram, Sham surreptitiously sprinkled a handful of salt into the glass of pure water that Ram was about to drink. Ram, accustomed to quenching his thirst with water after his meal, unknowingly took a sip. The moment the salt touched his taste buds, a wave of bitterness engulfed him, and he almost retched. The water had turned unbearably acrid.

Disgusted by the taste, Ram hastily poured the saline concoction into a large pot of fresh water. Curiously, after a while, he fetched a ladle of water from the same pot and took a sip. To his amazement, it wasn't as bitter as before. Ram was baffled by this paradox. How could the same quantity of salt, when mixed into the pure water in a big jar, not taste bitter?

Perplexed by this puzzle, Ram decided to seek the counsel of the village's revered head priest. This priest was renowned for his profound wisdom and his knack for imparting invaluable life lessons through simple parables.

Ram shared his plan with Sham, inviting him to join the journey to meet the head priest.

Although Sham was busy playing with his numerous schoolmates, they all agreed to accompany Ram to meet the wise head priest of their village.

As the group of friends made their way to the village temple where the wise head priest resided, Ram couldn't help but ponder over the strange incident with the salted water. He wondered if there was a deeper meaning behind it, something more than just a prank played by his friend Sham. Upon reaching the temple, they found the head priest sitting peacefully under a massive old tree, surrounded by flowers and incense. The priest, known for his serene demeanor and insightful guidance, welcomed them with a warm smile.

Ram explained the incident to the priest, describing how the water in the glass tasted incredibly bitter when it was mixed with salt, but when poured into the big jar filled with fresh water, the bitterness disappeared. He asked the priest for an explanation.

The wise priest listened attentively and then nodded in understanding. He began to explain, "My dear children, life often presents us with situations that are similar to your experience with the salty water. Life's challenges and adversities can make us feel bitter and unpalatable, much like the water in the glass. However, just as the water became bearable when mixed with a larger source of fresh water in the jar, our own bitterness can be diluted and made more manageable when we surround ourselves with positivity, love, and good company."

He continued, "In this world, we encounter many 'Shams' who may try to trick us, deceive us, or bring negativity into our lives. But if we choose to be like the 'lake' and not the 'glass,' we can overcome these challenges. A lake has a vast expanse and depth, and it doesn't let the bitterness of a single incident affect its entire being. It absorbs and dilutes the bitterness, just as the jar of fresh water did."

Ram and his friends listened intently, understanding the profound lesson the head priest was imparting. The priest concluded, "So, my dear children, always strive to be like a lake, deep and expansive in your heart. Surround yourself with positivity, good friends, and a sense of purpose, and you'll find that life's challenges become more bearable. Don't let a single incident or negativity define you, for you have the power to dilute the bitterness and keep moving forward with grace and strength."

Ram and his friends left the temple with a newfound understanding of life's challenges and the importance of resilience, positivity, and the support of good friends. They decided to be like the lake, embracing life's ups and downs with open hearts and a willingness to overcome adversity, just as a vast lake absorbs and dilutes the bitterness of a single glass of salted water.

21. We are Powerful

The story unfolds on a warm, bustling street corner in a quaint neighbourhood. The old egg seller sits there, a weathered face etched with years of struggle. His cart is laden with a modest collection of eggs, each one a symbol of his toil. The sun casts long shadows as he waits, hopeful that today will bring a better fortune than the ones that have lately eluded him. He watches the world pass by, people of various backgrounds and walks of life, all navigating their own journeys.

Then enters our protagonist, an affluent woman whose demeanor exudes confidence and power. She approaches the egg seller with a sense of entitlement, her designer sunglasses concealing the judgment in her eyes. She asks about the price of the eggs, and the seller, with a mixture of weariness and hope, answers her inquiry with a simple, "Rs. 5/- an egg, Madam."

The negotiation that ensues is not just a matter of haggling over a few rupees; it is a clash of worlds. The woman, seemingly unaware of the old man's struggles, decides to exercise her power. She proposes a deal, challenging the price set by the egg seller. "I will take 6 eggs for Rs. 25/-," she declares, making it clear that her terms are non-negotiable, and she threatens to walk away if not met. The seller, feeling the weight of financial desperation, reluctantly agrees to her conditions, his eyes betraying his disappointment.

As the woman leaves, she feels a sense of triumph, believing she has outsmarted the old seller. The eggs sit nestled in her bag as she gets into her luxurious car, parked just steps away, and heads to a posh restaurant to meet a friend. The restaurant is a stark contrast to the humble street corner. Crystal chandeliers glisten, and the aroma of gourmet dishes wafts through the air. The menu, adorned with foreign names and exotic ingredients, is an entirely different world from the cart of eggs.

The two friends indulge themselves, ordering an extravagant feast. They sample a bit of everything but leave much untouched. As the bill arrives, the woman takes out her wallet and pays the hefty sum of Rs. 1,400/-. However, when it comes to the tip, she leaves a generous Rs. 1,500/-, instructing the owner to keep the change. The restaurant owner, while grateful for the unexpected tip, cannot help but feel slightly perplexed, as his establishment does not rely on such acts of generosity to survive.

The story underscores a recurring paradox in society: why do we, as individuals, often choose to wield our power when bargaining with those in need, seeking to maximize our own gain? And why is our generosity more abundant when dealing with people who are already well-off, those who do not necessarily require our benevolence?

The poignant message, as articulated by the narrator, resonates throughout the narrative. It underscores the importance of compassion and the idea that acts of charity should be wrapped in dignity, preserving the self-respect of those receiving the aid.

In conclusion, "WE ARE POWERFUL" is a powerful reminder that our actions can impact the lives of others in ways we may not always realize. It urges us to reflect on the choices we make and to recognize that true power lies in the ability to uplift and empower those in need while preserving their dignity.

22.The secret of Happiness.

There's a well-known tale of an Indian boy in pursuit of the secret to happiness. His quest led him to a humble monk residing in a village, widely admired by its inhabitants. This monk, living a simple life in a mud and husk hut, was devoid of negative emotions and held love for everyone. He was an embodiment of unparalleled happiness. The boy approached the monk, seeking to unravel the secret of this happiness. The monk, surprised by the earnest question from a young boy, grappled with how to convey such profound wisdom to someone of such tender age. After careful thought, the monk proposed a solution.

He said to the boy, "Come, my son, I will share with you the secret of happiness under one condition. You must take a tour of the entire village, observing its people, the beauty of the surroundings, the residents' way of life, and everything in between." Handing the boy a spoon filled with water, the monk instructed him to keep the water from spilling while exploring the village.

The child, viewing the task as simple, eagerly agreed and began his journey. With youthful vigor, he swiftly completed the tour. Upon returning, he proudly informed the monk of his accomplishment. Smiling, the monk inquired, "What did you notice on the first street of the village? Did you see the houses where the people reside?" Regretfully, the boy replied, "I'm sorry, sir. I was entirely focused on safeguarding the water in the spoon. My attention was solely on this crucial task, and I couldn't observe anything else. As requested, I completed the full round without spilling a drop of water."

"No, you haven't fulfilled your complete duty. You neglected to observe the village as instructed. You must take another tour of the village and return to me with a comprehensive report detailing all its aspects." The boy consented and completed a second round of the village, presenting a detailed account to the monk. He was content, having taken in every detail about the village, and elaborated it to the monk.

"But where is the water?" questioned the monk. "Sir, I was so engrossed in observing the village that I failed to tend to the water, and it spilled from the spoon," the boy admitted. Once again, he was deemed to have failed in his task.

The child sank into a state of despair, tears flowing at his inability to discover the secret of happiness. The monk approached, embraced him affectionately, and explained that he hadn't failed in his duty; rather, he failed to grasp the lesson on happiness concealed within his task.

The monk further elucidated, "You were entrusted with two duties: to observe the village's beauty and to safeguard the water in the spoon. While focusing on the water, you neglected the village, and while engrossed in observing the village, you overlooked the water. You needed to maintain a balance between both tasks. It was this equilibrium of duties that eluded you in your task. We have the right to relish the world's beauty and pleasures, but we must also fulfil our responsibilities."

He continued, "We must strike a balance between caring for our duties at home, work, with our parents, children, and everything else. At times, we forget to appreciate life's beauty, getting lost in the rush of a hectic world. At other times, we neglect our responsibilities. For a content life, balance is crucial. Family, work, health, enjoyment, and responsibilities are all equally significant. Creating and maintaining this equilibrium is vital for a fulfilling life."

23. Story: Mullah Nasruddin in Paradise

Once, the renowned Mulla Nasruddin pondered the potential luxuries and comforts awaiting in paradise. In his dream, he envisioned a realm of lavish opulence, where every desire was effortlessly fulfilled merely by thinking about it. He found himself in awe as he discovered that sumptuous dishes appeared before him upon mere contemplation.

Amazed at this miraculous manifestation, Nasruddin's rational mind led him to question the feasibility of such spontaneous food creation. Instantly, the table laden with delicacies vanished. Regretting his cynicism, he longed for the food to reappear, and it did. Satisfying his hunger, he then yearned for a drink, and his favorite wine materialized, much to his delight.

Satiated by the feast, drowsiness set in, prompting him to seek a place to rest. As he reclined, he speculated about the entity orchestrating this paradise. Convinced it couldn't be the work of a mere mortal, he mused on the involvement of otherworldly forces, considering the possibility of ghosts. Suddenly, as he entertained this thought, terrifying ghosts materialized exactly as he had envisioned. Overwhelmed with fear, Nasruddin worried the ghosts would expel him from paradise. In an instant, they seized him by the legs and ejected him from this dream paradise.

Upon awakening from his reverie, Nasruddin shared with his wife the profound realization that our thoughts construct the world we inhabit, and we receive according to what we believe we deserve.

This tale extends beyond mere amusement; stripped of its enchantment and exaggeration, it offers a reflection on the mechanics of life.

Our thoughts serve as the initial seeds of our actions, channeling our creativity. It falls upon us to steer and cultivate our thoughts towards constructive paths. Their potency is profound and often dictates the eventual outcome. Essentially, the results we envision tend to materialize based on our predominant thoughts, be they positive or negative—this is within our control.

The grand achievements of eminent figures weren't swift victories; they dedicated years to methodically learning, encountering setbacks, and understanding the reasons for their failures. These experiences honed their skills, allowing them to realize their aspirations through persistent efforts and positive thinking. We all share this journey, aspiring for contentment. Our desires breed joy, fostering a positive mindset that enhances our ability to discern the good in people and situations. This shift in perspective cultivates a more positive and joyful persona.

character and principles, might resist picking up bad habits despite being amidst negative influences.

Yet, the societal perspective remains pivotal. While it's possible to remain untainted by bad company, the majority of society will judge individuals by the company they keep. Even if one maintains goodness in the presence of negativity, society might not empathize or understand. The company one keeps often shapes how they are perceived by others.

26. Story: Greed prevails upon ethics

Once, I came across a humorous Punjabi poem within the pages of a book titled "Bhaiya Once More" (Bhaiya, meaning an elder man and a renowned Punjabi poet). The poem conveys a valuable moral lesson:

In a quaint village in Punjab, India, there dwelled a humble and virtuous man. He was content with his modest means, a paragon of honesty and moral integrity. He never resorted to deceit for personal gain, finding immense satisfaction in the simple life he shared with his wife. One fine day, after toiling in the fields, his employer rewarded him with a cash incentive of Rs. 50, a sum he had never possessed before. His joy was contagious, and his wife, who had longed for stuffed potato bread, seized the opportunity to request her husband to purchase some potatoes from a nearby vendor.

Eager to share his newfound happiness, the poor man readily agreed to buy the potatoes. As he set off on this errand, he noticed a wallet discarded in a corner of the road. Filled with curiosity, he picked up the wallet and conducted a thorough search, leading to his astonishment as he discovered a stack of currency notes within. Overflowing with gratitude, he knelt to touch the hallowed earth, offering thanks to the Almighty for this unexpected boon. To him, this windfall was not merely a wallet brimming with money; it represented his fortune.

His imagination soared as he envisioned the grand possibilities this money held. With it, he planned to purchase land, hire laborers, and establish his own agricultural venture. He dreamed of constructing a magnificent house, adorning his wife in fine attire, and mingling in society as an esteemed gentleman. No longer would he be a daily wage earner; he would ascend to the status of a landlord.

Contemplating the repercussions of losing the found money, the man wrestled with his conscience. He pondered the potential suffering of the person who lost such a substantial amount. Realizing the money wasn't rightfully his, a sense of responsibility and moral duty emerged within him. His conscience pricked him, insisting that he had no right to keep the money; it belonged to its rightful owner. He grappled with conflicting thoughts: his mind urged him to enjoy the windfall, branding it as a stroke of luck, while his inner voice admonished against succumbing to greed.

Amid this inner turmoil, he sought guidance through prayer, imploring his higher power for direction. Upon introspection, he found clarity: the money was not his to keep, and he had a moral obligation to return it. Following this resolve, he promptly visited a nearby police station, surrendering the wallet and its contents, urging them to ensure its return to the rightful owner.

On his way back, he stopped to purchase potatoes for his wife. Despite his recent moral dilemma about the rightful ownership of money, when faced with the opportunity, the temptation of two potatoes overcame him. In a moment of weakness, he succumbed to theft, swiping the potatoes without the vendor's notice.

This stark contrast highlights the complexities of human behavior: a person committed to honesty and ethical living is willing to relinquish unearned possessions for peace of mind. Yet, when entangled in the web of greed, even the smallest opportunity can lead to unethical actions. The man's shift from righteousness to theft, regardless of the insignificant value, brought forth consequences of humiliation, punishment, and societal stigma. Imprisonment tarnished his reputation, causing the loss of respect and trust, ultimately leaving him ostracized within society.

27. Impact of Small Gestures

During challenging times, it often feels like everything is working against our desires. Our work environment, family life, mental state, and emotions all endure periods of desolation and distress. Every task seems arduous and daunting. It's natural in such moments to feel anxious, lose patience, and be overcome by fear and insecurity. This state often leads to an inclination towards anger, causing us to disregard human values, moral ethics, and overlook many significant aspects.

Conversely, during more routine or favorable phases of life when things align with our wishes, why do we tend to overlook the importance of small details? We often neglect the significance of minor matters, daily habits, and simple courtesies, solely focusing on major accomplishments. While we expend our energy in pursuit of grand objectives, we forget that it's the cumulative effect of small things, minor actions, and daily decisions that shape us into dignified individuals, earning respect and love from those around us.

Gestures such as showing respect to our subordinates, honoring our elders, and extending a helping hand to those in need significantly contribute to the establishment of our identity, one that's acknowledged and esteemed by others. While monumental goals remain our ultimate targets, the path to achieving these aspirations is paved with numerous small efforts and decisions. It's these seemingly inconsequential actions that ultimately define our character, shape our personality, and showcase our capacity for selflessness. Below, I've included an inspiring anecdote written by the former South African President, Mr. Nelson Mandela, illustrating the power of such smaller acts.

Story: Nelson Mandela

Upon assuming the presidency, I once invited some members of my close protection team to accompany me on a stroll through the city for lunch at a local restaurant. Seated in one of the downtown eateries, we placed our orders and awaited our meals.

As our orders arrived, I noticed a man sitting nearby, patiently waiting for his food. Moved by a sense of inclusion, I instructed one of my security guards to invite the man to join us for a meal. Following my request, the guard approached the man, who timidly accepted, took his food, and joined me at the table. Throughout his meal, his hands trembled incessantly, and beads of sweat dotted his brow. After he finished his food, he quietly departed.

Observing the man's apparent illness, one of the guards remarked on his trembling hands. I shared with them that the man was not unwell, but rather, he was one of the prison guards from the institution where I spent many years. I recounted the history, how during my days of torment and suffering in prison, after pleading for a sip of water, this same guard, instead of providing water, would douse me with his own urine. This traumatic memory caused the man to tremble in my presence, expecting retribution now that I held the position of President.

However, revenge is not part of my character or ethical beliefs. I explained that retaliatory actions tear down nations, while the spirit of tolerance builds them.

This narrative underlines the significance of small gestures, actions, and habits in influencing our lives. Often, we overlook the impact of these seemingly inconsequential elements that actually shape the trajectory of our existence. We tend to disregard their importance, mistakenly believing that only grand endeavors can drive change, failing to recognize that it is these small, often overlooked details that pave the way toward achieving significant goals.

28. POWER OF LANGUAGE

In the bustling town of Brightsworth, a place where the power of language was as palpable as the air they breathed, lived three friends: Alana, Marcus, and Eva. Their lives were intertwined by the enchanting yet formidable force of words.

Alana, with her captivating yet tactless manner, often spoke in sharp, biting tones. She found herself entangled in conflicts due to her abrasive language. One sunny day, she encountered a lost puppy in the park. Feeling frustrated and inconvenienced, she yelled at the scared pup, demanding it to go away. Her harsh words left the puppy cowering in fear, illustrating the detrimental impact of sharp and unkind language.

Marcus, the ever-charming orator, possessed the gift of articulation that left listeners enchanted. He approached life with a gentle yet persuasive demeanor. In an effort to mend fences between feuding neighbors, Marcus used soothing and conciliatory words. His words, filled with empathy and kindness, dissolved the tension, bringing about a serene reconciliation.

Eva, known for her encouraging and supportive nature, understood the strength of affirmative language. She encountered a struggling artist at the local fair, disheartened by the lack of appreciation for his work. With her encouraging words, she uplifted his spirit, praising his creativity and talent. Her supportive language kindled a spark of inspiration, reigniting his passion for art.

As time passed, the three friends encountered a dilemma in their community. A dispute over a proposed development project divided the townsfolk. Alana, fueled by her penchant for brash language, spoke fervently and disparagingly, aggravating the situation and igniting conflict. Marcus, utilizing his persuasive and soothing words, attempted to calm the escalating tensions. His eloquent speeches managed to pacify some but fell short in uniting the opposing factions.

Eva, recognizing the need for positivity, chose words that resonated with encouragement and optimism. With her gentle yet compelling tone, she emphasized common ground and mutual benefit. Her words, a blend of empathy and hope, acted as a soothing balm, bringing people together and fostering a spirit of collaboration.

Ultimately, the power of language was demonstrated vividly through their experiences. Alana's abrasive language, though potent, sowed discord, while Marcus's persuasive words had a calming effect. However, it was Eva's affirming and unifying language that brought about a resolution, showcasing the profound impact of words when used positively.

The trio learned a valuable lesson from their experiences. The tone, intent, and choice of words held the transformative ability to either escalate tensions or nurture harmony. They realized that while sharp words might leave wounds, sweet and encouraging language had the power to heal and unify, leaving an enduring impact on the lives of those they touched.

The story of Alana, Marcus, and Eva carries several valuable messages for the young generation, emphasizing the immense impact of language and the choices one makes when communicating:

Awareness of Words' Power: Young individuals should understand and acknowledge the potent influence of language. Words possess the power to shape relationships, inspire change, and impact the world around them. By recognizing this influence, they can use their words more thoughtfully and responsibly.

Importance of Kindness and Empathy: The story illustrates the significance of choosing kind and empathetic words. By embracing positivity and empathy in their language, the younger generation can foster understanding, bridge divides, and create a more harmonious environment, whether in personal interactions or larger societal contexts.

Tone and Intent Matter: It's essential for the youth to be mindful of their tone and intent when communicating. The way they convey their thoughts can affect how their messages are received. Choosing a tone that's gentle, respectful, and considerate can help in building stronger connections and resolving conflicts peacefully.

Impact of Encouragement: Encouraging and supportive words have the power to uplift others, inspire creativity, and kindle motivation. Young individuals can learn to be supportive and appreciative of others' efforts, boosting their confidence and fostering a positive environment.

Resolution through Collaboration: Collaborative and unifying language can bring people together. Encouraging dialogue, finding common ground, and fostering an atmosphere of collaboration rather than conflict leads to stronger relationships and more effective solutions.

The Power of Choice: The story demonstrates that individuals have the power to choose their words and the impact thóse words have on others. Young people can realize that they have a choice in how they communicate and the effect their language can have on their relationships and society as a whole.

In conclusion, the tale underscores the significant impact that language and communication have on the world. The message to the young generation is clear: use words wisely, thoughtfully, and with kindness to create a positive and harmonious environment, both personally and within the broader community. Their words and actions have the power to shape the world around them, and by choosing positivity and empathy, they can make a meaningful difference in the lives of others.

How our language can make a difference :-

Empowerment through Learning: The story demonstrates the empowerment that comes from learning and applying knowledge. It encourages individuals, especially the younger generation, to embrace learning as a tool for personal growth and problem-solving.

Problem-Solving and Innovation: It emphasizes the importance of critical thinking, innovation, and creativity in applying knowledge to resolve challenges. Encouraging the youth to think creatively and seek solutions through learning and exploration.

The Transformative Power of Education: Education and the quest for knowledge are depicted as powerful tools that can bring about significant and positive changes. It underlines the message that education is a catalyst for progress and transformation in society.

Positive Impact on Communities: The story highlights the impact of knowledge on communities. It suggests that individuals who apply their knowledge for the greater good can create positive changes that benefit society as a whole.

Belief in Potential: It instills a belief in the potential of individuals to make a difference through their pursuit of knowledge. It encourages the younger generation to believe in their capacity to bring about change through the understanding and application of what they learn.

A Call to Action: The story serves as a call to action, urging young individuals to embrace education, be curious, and use their knowledge to address challenges and contribute positively to their surroundings.

In summary, the story's message is a testament to the transformative power of knowledge, underscoring its role in personal growth, problem-solving, and contributing to the betterment of society. It encourages individuals, especially the young, to embrace learning and apply their knowledge as a means to unlock opportunities and create positive change in the world around them.

****